D0422114

Christmas Beer

Christmas Beer

The Cheeriest, Tastiest, and Most Unusual Holiday Brews

by Don Russell

Photographs by Everett W. Faircloth

UNIVERSE

For Theresa and Christmas night.

First published in the United States of America in 2008
by Universe Publishing, A Division of
Rizzoli International Publications, Inc.
300 Park Avenue South
New York, NY 10010
www.rizzoliusa.com

2008 2009 2010 2011 / 10 9 8 7 6 5 4 3 2 1

Distributed in the U.S. trade by Random House, New York

Design by Paul Kepple, Headcase Design

Printed in China

ISBN-13: 978-0-7893-1796-4

Library of Congress Control Number: 2008903947

CONTENTS

THE STORY OF CHRISTMAS BEER 7

  'Tis the Season 9

  The Spirits of Christmas Past 13

  The Ancient Yuletide Carol 17

  A Right Jolly Old Elf 21

  On, Comet! On, Cupid! On, Donder . . . and Fritz! 24

  Tidings of Comfort and Juleøl 29

  Joy to the World 33

  Oy! Holy Night 41

  Ho, Ho, Hic! 43

  Santa Lives 47

  O, Little Town of Bethlehem, Pennsylvania 51

THE WORLD'S 50 BEST CHRISTMAS BEERS 55

MORE BEERS TO ENJOY FOR CHRISTMAS 131

SOME RECIPES AND PRACTICAL INFO 181

  Collect 'Em, Drink 'Em 194

  Serving Up a Holiday Brew 198

  Style Notes 201

  Defining Beer Styles 203

Acknowledgments 205

Index 206

The Story of
CHRISTMAS BEER

'TIS THE SEASON

The children were nestled all snug in their beds,
While visions of sugarplums danced in their heads.

Like most beer drinkers, I'm still a kid at heart. Drinking a good brew mainly is just fun—nothing more, nothing less. Crack one open, put up your feet, and take a long pull: this simple act is as joyous as playing stickball on the street corner or skipping school on a warm afternoon was for me as a kid.

I don't mean to diminish the importance of my favorite beverage. A great beer is more than just a glass of suds. It's full of character and nuance; it's the product of careful craftsmanship; it's a vital part of our cuisine; it's a reflection of culture and history. Yet even as I value all of this, drinking a beer at its best reminds me of how I felt about the Spalding basketball Santa Claus brought me on Christmas Day when I was about seven years old: I didn't know how to play the game, I couldn't reach the hoop, but I could bounce that thing all day, just for fun.

Ah, Christmas. Remember the fun? The pure, unrestrained, completely positive energy of the day?

When I was a kid, I couldn't wait for Christmas morning. No way could I ever get to sleep. The night before, I would be a maniac, inspecting my stocking for holes, taste-testing the cookies for Santa, checking the midnight sky for signs of Rudolph. Sugarplums? Forget them—if I managed to fall asleep, I was dreaming of a new Matchbox car or Rock 'Em Sock 'Em Robots.

The truth is, I'm still the same way about Christmas. Only these days the gift I dream about is beer—or more precisely, Christmas beer.

And no, I don't mean a box of Bud wrapped in red and green. Christmas beers are ales and lagers made by breweries around the world once a year, as a gift to all of us kids at heart. Full of flavor, they often contain secret ingredients; typically, they have a bit more alcohol, for a nice way to settle in to a long winter's nap.

When I first started drinking beer in the seventies, I remember just one holiday beer: Noche Buena from Dos Equis. It was a slightly darker lager, a bit sweeter, a nice treat. There may have been a few others around, but I never encountered them at home in Philadelphia.

Today it's a completely different scene. Hundreds of beautifully decorated Christmas labels line the store shelves during the holidays. Often the beers are packaged in oversized, corked bottles—a festive gift for holiday parties. Many are traditional European lagers whose roots go back centuries. Still more are modern, handcrafted ales made by innovative American brewers who don't hesitate to experiment with offbeat ingredients. There are ales spiced with cinnamon, sweetened with honey, or flavored with unusual hops varieties—no two are the same.

Indeed, unlike other beer varieties—say, India pale ale, porter, or bock—Christmas beer does not represent a specific style. There are no rules, no brewing guidelines. Christmas beer is whatever a brewer wants to make—as long as it's special. And that's what makes the holidays so much fun for beer drinkers. Like kids who anticipate the presents under the tree, those of us with a thirst for malt and hops know there's something good inside those bottles, just waiting to be opened.

For me, a big part of the fun is also the search for these gifts: the annual Christmas beer run. Blame it on restrictive state laws or quirky distribution deals, but you can never be entirely certain where—or even if—you'll find your favorites. Some are brewed in such limited quantities that you practically have to be waiting at the brewery gates to get a taste.

So every year I pick a day in early December to skip work and go beer hunting. One year I flew to Norway for its holiday beer, juleøl. In other years, I've trooped off to the West Coast. Most years, though, I stay on the East Coast for a beer-hunting expedition can last twelve hours and take me through five states, plus the District of Columbia. Usually, the local deli will have a few dependable selections from big breweries: Sierra Nevada Celebration, Anheuser-Busch Winter's Bourbon Cask Ale. Another nearby distributor helpfully mixes twenty-four different microbrews into a case. A local specialty store always carries rare Champagne-sized bottles from Belgium.

I remember one epic beer run during an early blizzard a few years ago when I stuffed my car trunk with no fewer than sixty different bottles. These were truly exceptional brands, like Scaldis Noël with its glittering snowscape label, the fantastically hoppy Three Floyds Alpha Klaus, and a bottle of St. Feuillien Cuvée de Noël that had already been aged for a year. But as much as I treasured these finds, it was a short visit to a northern Virginia brewpub that made this beer run so memorable.

Just off a busy highway in a suburban shopping center, the lights of Sweetwater Tavern had beckoned me through the snowfall. I was tired of driving, and the place was serving something called Happy Trails Christmas Ale. The bartender slid a pint glass in front of me; the rim was crusted with brown sugar, spices, and crushed pumpkin seeds. I took a sip and felt a quick rush of warmth. But it was not from the beer. In the dining room, an office party had just broken into song: "God Rest Ye Merry Gentlemen." The entire bar joined in the carol.

The Christmas spirit truly is never more alive than when you share it with your fellow man.

My wife and I share a holiday tradition at home. We open our gifts to each other on Christmas night. Alone in front of the fireplace, with music on the stereo, it's our moment to relax after the mad rush of holiday shopping and parties. In our first years of marriage, we always split a single cobalt-blue bottle of Samuel Adams Triple Bock, a powerfully strong, maple-flavored lager that is sipped, like port. Our bottles of that classic beer are long gone, but when I head down to the basement now I know I'll find a bottle (or two, or three) of Christmas beer. Maybe it's Brasserie Dupont Avec les Bons Voeux, a saison-style ale from Belgium that has hints of honey. Or perhaps it's River Horse Belgian Frostbite, made up the river from us in Lambertville, New Jersey.

I'll be honest, I can never remember what we have.

And that's not the beer talking. It's the spirit of the holiday, of surprise and sharing, of happiness and love. Of feeling like a kid on Christmas Day. And having fun.

THE SPIRITS OF CHRISTMAS PAST

Drooling Elf. Sled Wrecker. Tannen Bomb. Wreck the Halls. Winterizer. From the tap list at your local brewpub to the shelves of beer stores across America, the holiday spirit is alive and in your face. Brewers vie for your attention with an assortment of tap handles and labels that boast of secret ingredients and potent strength: Happy Holidaze, Frosty's Revenge, Yule Be Sorry. You can't help but wonder: is this really the spirit of Christmas?

In fact, winter beer may be more true to the celebration than Santa Claus himself. All that stuff about tinsel and gifts, wreaths and holly, and stockings hung by the chimney with care? That all came later. Beer—strong beer—is the very essence of this important holiday. It is quite literally the spirit of Christmas.

> *"Our bellys then let us prepare*
> *to drink some Christmas beer."*
> —FROM *"Merry Boys of Christmas,"* AN ENGLISH BALLAD OF 1660

So uncork a bottle of Delirium Noël, and let me tell you the real story of Christmas celebrations.

It begins well before the birth of Christ, before the Greek and Roman, Norse, Egyptian deities, before paganism.

It begins with the sun.

To early man, the sun was god. The sun gave the earth its warmth, its light, its life. Perhaps during the Stone Age, but certainly by the Neolithic period about 3300 BC, man was worshipping the sun through daily ritual.

In Ireland's County Meath, for example, stands a five-thousand-year-old structure called Newgrange. Estimated to be older than the Great Pyra-

OPPOSITE PAGE: Yes, Virginia, Santa drinks! In this ad from the 1920s, he's going for the hard stuff.

mid of Giza and Stonehenge, it offers clear evidence of early sun worshipping. Just after dawn on a few days surrounding the winter solstice, when the sun is at its lowest point in the sky, a beam of sunlight penetrates a carefully constructed rooftop opening, shining down a long corridor and illuminating an interior chamber. For a brief time, the room is lit and reveals symbols carved on the wall. Was it built mainly for worshipping? or a ceremony? as simply a burial site? No one knows. But its importance is that it marks the shortest day of the year, the solstice, the day that the sun—sacred god herself—returns and the earth is reborn.

> *"Dear Santa,*
> *I'll leave you a glass of ginger ale, and if you're still thirsty, I could leave you two quarts of beer. Remember, my house is the one with the beer.*
> *Love, Cindy"*
> —LETTER TO SANTA FOUND IN THE
> RUTLAND, VERMONT, SANTA CLAUS MAILBOX, 1959

Can there be any other day more worthy of celebration? Evidence of solstice festivals is found in our earliest recorded history. People gathered. The harvest was complete. The beer was fermented.

Yes, the beer. Nearly as soon as man learned to grow grain, he—or, more likely, the women in the family—was also making beer. Some archeologists believe beer is the reason man evolved from his nomadic ways; he needed to settle down to raise the crops that became the substance of this filling drink. Six thousand years ago, the Sumerians of Mesopotamia, the earliest known civilization, were filling their vessels with a bready ale. But fermentation was still a mystery, one that wouldn't be solved for millennia. The drink was considered to be a gift of nature, of the gods. It was filling, it was healthy, and it was safer to drink than untreated water.

And if you drank enough, you just might see god.

Surely, on the occasion of the solstice, this gift would have flowed freely, a bond between man and the gods, between earth and sun.

Later civilizations built their own mythologies, many centering on the sun. The ancient Mesopotamians worshipped Utu, the sun god. The Aztecs had Tonatiuh, or "He Who Goes Forth Shining." The Egyptians bowed to Ra, the Greeks built temples to Helios, the Celts believed in Lugh, "the Shining One." Often, the birth of these gods (and others) would be celebrated around the winter solstice. By the time of Christ, the most widely celebrated feast was Saturnalia, in honor of the Roman god of harvest, Saturn. It was a week of feasting, from December 17 to 25, when businesses were shut down, slaves and owners exchanged roles, gifts were given, clothing was optional, and drunkenness abounded. The first-century-BC poet Catullus would call it *Saturnalibus, optimo dierum*—which, if I remember my high school Latin, means "party time."

What does all of this have to do with Christmas?

In the earliest days of Christianity, the birth of Christ was of little importance. It was his martyrdom, not the nativity, that was the cause of adulation. No one knew the date of his birth; it might not even have been in December.

Meanwhile, in third-century Rome, the emperor Aurelian sought to establish a religion around a single deity—Sol, the sun god. A festival in his honor, Dies Natalis Solis Invicti ("the birthday of the unconquered sun"), fell on December 25. A century later, Pope Julius I would choose that very day as the official date of Christ's birth.

Was the choice of that date divine? Or was it a calculated ploy to usurp the pagans' cherished holiday? It doesn't matter. The impact on the world was the same. Traditions surrounding the solstice festivals—gift giving, feasting, role-swapping, and, yes, beer drinking—were transferred to the celebration of Christmas.

The Christian doctrine spread, promoted by disciples and formalized with the establishment of hundreds of monasteries throughout Europe. The Trappist monks were guided by the rules of St. Benedict, who wrote, "You are only really a monk when you live from the work of your hands." Self-sufficiency was their hallmark. They grew their own crops, baked their own bread—and made their own beer. And when the monks celebrated the birth of their Lord, they raised cups of their finest, their strongest beer—just as the solstice celebrants had centuries before. In the twelfth century, Francis of Assisi scoffed at the idea of abstaining on Christmas Day—even if it fell on a Friday, a day of fasting. Deny the role of beer in Christmas at your own folly.

And yet, through the ages, some have suggested there is no room for alcohol on so sacred a day. They have a point. By the seventeenth century, Christmas Day had evolved into a blowout, with raging drunks—fueled by distilled spirits—taking over the streets in Europe and America. The wassail tradition (see p. 17) was becoming little more than an excuse for the lower classes to raise hell and demand money from the wealthy. In the early years of the Massachusetts Bay Colony, for example, the Reverend Increase Mather griped that colonists "are consumed in Compotations, in Interludes, in playing at Cards, in Revellings, in excess of Wine, in mad Mirth. . . ." The stiff-collars banned Christmas in 1659 in Massachusetts.

But the "Revellings" continued. By the American Revolution, it was the custom throughout the states to brew and enjoy what one early American historian called "a right strong Christmas beer." When Santa finally arrived on the scene in the mid-nineteenth century, he was often portrayed with a beer in hand. Even during Prohibition, the holiday was celebrated with bootleg ale. And when the nation finally came to its senses, the president rushed the repeal of Prohibition through Congress so Americans would have beer in time for the holidays.

A right strong beer. Sled Wrecker, Tannen Bomb—this is Christmas beer, brewed potent to raise the spirits, brewed as a gift from the gods in honor of the sun . . . in honor of the Son.

In the second half of the first millennium, it wasn't Christmas that Christians celebrated so widely, but rather the Epiphany, the date that marks the visit of the Magi to the infant Jesus. With a nod toward that festival, Belgium's Alvinne brewery produces a trio of ales called Gaspar, Balthazar, and Melchior, named for the three wise men.

THE ANCIENT YULETIDE CAROL

Marin Brewing makes a Christmas beer with nutmeg, mace, cinnamon, vanilla, and orange peel. Lakefront Holiday Spice contains orange zest and clove. Bethlehem Brew Works flavors its Rude Elf's Reserve with sweet gale and allspice. Nutmeg? Allspice? Is this an ale, or a slice of pumpkin pie?

As my mom used to admonish me, don't turn up your nose till you take a bite.

And when you finally have a glass, you might be surprised to learn that this is the way beer tasted thousands of years ago. It wasn't until the 1500s that brewers seeking to balance the sweet flavor of sugary malt settled on hops, bitter, aromatic buds that grow on vines. Before that, they used anything they could find: tree bark, flowers, even poisonous mushrooms. Only for special occasions such as weddings, baptisms, or feasts would they break out the exotic spices: cinnamon from China, mace from the East Indies, black pepper from Thailand.

Perhaps it was a cup of spiced ale that Rowena, the fifth-century Saxon temptress, raised as she seduced Vortigen, the Briton warlord. Legend has it she toasted him, *Ves heill, Hlaford Cyning*—"Good health, Lord King." Rowena got her man, and the Saxons got their kingdom. And for centuries after, the Anglo-Saxons raised their drinking cups with the same words: *Ves heill!*

Wassail!

Over the centuries the toast evolved through northern Europe into a custom that might seem familiar today. At Christmas, well-wishers banging drums and carrying cups decorated with ribbons would visit nearby farmers, wishing them good luck on the next year's crops. The grateful farmer greeted the noisy crew with bowls of ale flavored with spice. Within the towns, it was the same joyful party, with merrymakers going door to door with their empty cups. The entire tradition—the cup, the greetings, the drink itself—became known as wassail. Today we might call it caroling.

> *"A mug of your Christmas Ale, sir*
> *Will make us merry and sing*
> *But money in our pockets*
> *Is much a better thing."*
> —FROM A NINETEENTH-CENTURY ENGLISH MUMMERS SONG

Indeed, the first Christmas carols were derived from wassails. Songs like "O Little Town of Bethlehem" and "Away in the Manger" floated through the streets long before they made their way into churches. However, to judge from the writings of Shakespeare and others, the earliest tunes often were a bit more raucous. One popular ditty opened:

Wisselton, wasselton, who lives here?
We've come to taste your Christmas beer

And not just any beer. Wassailers sought the very best ale. Another song demanded:

We want none of your pale beer, nor none of your small

A fitting wassail would be a strong English ale flavored with nutmeg and sugar, garnished with toast and roasted crab apples, and served perhaps with sweet cakes. Some called the beverage "lamb's wool," perhaps because it was so warming.

Bring food from off your table and beer from out o' your barrel
For if you don't, we'll stop and sing another ancient carol

After a couple stanzas, the carolers would be welcomed in; anything less wasn't only un-Christian, it risked bad luck. Typically, it was the poor who carried on the tradition the most avidly, turning up on the doorsteps of the rich, hoping for a drink and a few coins. This wasn't considered begging; instead, it stemmed from the long practice of feudal charity, with lords sharing some of their wealth with the peasants on holy days.

Only a Scrooge would (and, famously, did) chase them off.

Sadly, the tradition eventually died, partly because conservative Christians objected to drunken behavior on a holy day, and partly because the wassailers had become a public nuisance. In New England, it wasn't unheard of for groups of caroling hoodlums to vandalize houses that had closed their doors.

The contents of that old wassail bowl live on, however, in spicy winter warmers that are a familiar part of today's Christmas beer scene. Full Sail Brewing even calls its holiday ale Wassail.

Of course, you can still make it yourself (for details, see the recipe on p. 190). And as you stir the batch, hum along:

Here we come a-wassailing
Among the leaves so green,
Here we come a-wand'ring
So fair to be seen.
Love and joy come to you,
And to you your wassail, too.
And God bless you, and send you
*   A Happy New Year,*
And God send you a
*   Happy New Year.*

During the medieval Feast of Fools, usually held on the day after Christmas, drunken crowds—often in costume—would fill the churches and attend a mock service led by a phony priest. During the mass, the "priest" and the audience would exchange dirty jokes, and then pour back onto the streets for an impromptu parade.

Today you can see vestiges of the Feast of Fools in Philadelphia's Mummers Parade on New Year's Day.

A RIGHT JOLLY OLD ELF

Here's a gruesome little holiday tale your folks probably never told you as a kid.

Once upon a time, three children were playing in a field. It turned dark, and on the way home, they stopped at a butcher's shop. The shopkeeper welcomed them inside—and then murdered them, slicing them up and stuffing their bodies into a barrel of brine.

Lovely, huh? And what does this have to do with Christmas and beer?

Seven years after the murders, sometime in the early fourth century, the butcher was visited by Nicholas, the bishop of Myra, in what is now Turkey. Nicholas examined the inside of the barrel, saw the body parts, and told the children to rise. A miracle! The children were restored to life and everyone lived happily ever after.

The end.

Well, not really.

Nicholas died on December 6, AD 343, and since then, his legend has grown. There are stories of how his secret gifts to a poor Christian saved the man's three daughters from prostitution. In others, he's credited with protecting travelers. People prayed to him, and more miracles were attributed to him.

Nicholas was made a saint by public acclaim. Yes, he's that St. Nicholas. He has become a "people's saint," a protector of all types—clerks, brides, dock workers, even butchers. Greece has named him its patron saint.

And at some point, brewers—an ungodly bunch—began praying to him, too.

Now, there's no record that St. Nicholas was a beer drinker; in his part of the world, it's likely that wine would've been his favorite. Experts surmise brewers turned to him because of that barrel (the one he fished the kids out of). Creating new life from a vat—isn't that what brewers do? Others say it wasn't brine in that barrel, but beer.

While the origin of St. Nicholas's role as the patron saint of brewers may remain a mystery, surely it's only a small task for this religious icon. Over the centuries, the stories of his generosity were told and retold. Across Europe, believers prayed to him and celebrated the day of his demise with small gifts for children. His veneration spread to the New World. The Vikings dedicated a cathedral to him in Greenland. Columbus named a Haitian port after him. Dutch immigrants in New York, in particular, honored him as their patron saint—Sinterklaas.

You see where this is headed.

Fifteen hundred years after his death, St. Nicholas begins to morph into Santa Claus. In 1808, early American author Washington Irving wrote of him flying through the night, dropping gifts down the chimneys of his favorites in Knickerbocker's *History of New York*. Fifteen years later, Clement Clarke Moore gave him a sleigh led by eight tiny reindeer in "A Visit from St. Nicholas." And in the midst of our bloody civil war, Thomas Nast, the newspaper illustrator who gave us the Democratic donkey and Republican elephant, completed the transition, turning him into a fat, jolly, gift-giving elf.

St. Nicholas, the patron saint of brewers, is Santa Claus.

Which only leads me to wonder: why do kids leave him milk and cookies on Christmas Eve? A hearty ale would be far more appropriate.

SAINT NICK'S SIDEKICK

In Europe, where St. Nicholas Day is still widely celebrated, the saint is accompanied by a mean, dark man who punishes naughty children—the butcher. Naturally, brewers—naughty kids at heart—have made a number of beers in tribute to the sinister character.

In the Netherlands, Jantjes Bierbrouwerij makes both a Sinterklaas beer and one in honor of Zwarte Piet (Black Peter), known for stuffing naughty urchins into his sack.

In France, where he's known as Père Fouettard (the whipping father), Brasserie Henry in Bazincourt-sur-Saulx serves a special holiday brew called La Bière du Père Fouettard.

In Austria and Bavaria, red-tongued Krampus shackles disobedient kids and threatens to drag them straight to hell unless they behave. Assuming they survive childhood, adults can toast the evil character with a Krampus lager at Munich's Airbräu brewpub.

And in Haverhill, Massachusetts, the legend of Germany's Black Santa is fittingly recalled with a powerful black lager called Knecht Ruprecht, served by the Tap brewpub.

THE KING OF HOPS

Listen to the Muzak in shopping malls during the holiday season and you're bound to hear a version of the nineteenth-century carol "Good King Wenceslas." You might even recall the lyrics:

> *Good King Wenceslas looked out*
> *On the feast of Stephen*
>
> *When the snow lay round about*
> *Deep and crisp and even*

Did you ever wonder who the heck King Wenceslas was? Anyone who's ever enjoyed a glass of Pilsner Urquell, the original pils, owes the man a toast.

The good king was St. Wenceslas I, duke of Bohemia (907–935) and patron saint of the Czech Republic. It was during his short reign that the Bohemian hops industry was established. So treasured were the hops in making beer, the duke decreed that anyone caught removing hops cuttings from Bohemia would be executed.

No good deed ever goes unpunished. Wenceslas was later murdered by his own drunken brother.

Nearly four hundred years later, his namesake, King Wenceslas II, played an instrumental role in establishing the city of Pilsen, which became one of the world's greatest brewing cities.

ON, COMET! ON, CUPID!
ON, DONDER . . . AND FRITZ!

When you take a look at the shelves at your favorite beer store each December, it's hard to imagine that just thirty years ago Christmas beer was almost unheard-of in America. No spiced ales, no decorated bottles, no noël.

Instead, back then the aisles at grocery stores and distributors were dominated by lagers from giants like Anheuser-Busch and Schlitz, and the only nod toward the holidays was a stack of cartons decorated with red and green crepe paper. Occasionally a few small breweries packaged special beers for

Christmas, but they were rare, with a very limited distribution.

During the summer of 1975, though, a man who says "I've always felt half-Jewish" was rediscovering the Christmas beer tradition in San Francisco. His name: Fritz Maytag, scion of the washing-machine family, and the undisputed father of America's beer renaissance.

Ten years earlier, Maytag had purchased the decrepit, near-bankrupt Anchor Brewing Company almost on a whim. At the time, there was no such thing as a microbrew, and Maytag was laughed off by many as a dreamer for his plan to rebuild the brewery. Indeed, those early years were daunting, as Maytag did everything from stirring the kettle to delivering the kegs himself. But hard work, innovation, superior ingredients, and meticulous attention to brewing techniques turned the brewery around. By 1975, Maytag had restored the quality of the brewery's classic Anchor Steam beer, and was ready to turn his attention to more adventurous brews.

First came a dark, rich porter, then a malty barleywine. And then, a Christmas beer.

"I was aware of the tradition in medieval villages where they would make special beers for various festival days," Maytag says. "You'd have beers brewed for weddings, festivals, and other celebrations. And certainly you'd brew them for Christmas." It made sense that a small brewery that had been revived thanks to old-world beer-making techniques would rediscover the tradition of holiday beer. There was only one problem: Maytag didn't have a clue what it should taste like.

"The only holiday beers that I was aware of were one from John Koch's brewery in Dunkirk, New York, and Noche Buena from Mexico," he recalls. The former was a typical, bland 1950s lager, the latter was an amber Vienna-style lager, and neither provided much inspiration. "We knew we wanted to do something special, so we just decided, let's do an English ale," he continues. It would be an all-malt brown ale with Cascades hops added during the later stages of fermentation, a process known as dry hopping.

Initially, just a few hundred cases were produced, and the beer was sold in twelve-packs, with a discreet label. "It was designed to be as noncommercial as it could possibly be, so we wouldn't offend anyone," Maytag notes. "I knew perfectly well it was a bit naughty to mix a religious holiday with beer . . . but I don't think I've ever heard a single word of criticism from anyone." The following year, Maytag boldly labeled his holiday beer, "Merry Christmas and Happy New Year: Our Special Ale." It was decorated with a handsome evergreen, the giant sequoia—a Christmas tree. Every year since, a different hand-drawn tree has appeared on the label.

And beneath that label lies one of the biggest secrets in American craft brewing.

In 1987, to celebrate his wedding, Maytag crafted a bridal ale filled with herbs and spices. It was so tasty that the brewery decided to add spices to its holiday ale that winter—and has done so ever since. There's a different recipe each season, and neither Maytag nor any of his employees have ever revealed what's behind those mysterious flavors. Honey? Cinnamon? Nutmeg?

"We've never told anyone what's in our Christmas ale!" Maytag boasts. "It's nice to have a secret."

How about cloves?

"No! That's the only thing I'm going to say. There are no cloves in it, none. I'm tired of hearing about cloves!"

Wonder what the original Our Special Ale tasted like? You can get a good idea by cracking open a bottle of Anchor's Liberty Ale. The English-style ale is based on the 1983 Christmas beer recipe.

Oldies but Goodies

Though Our Special Ale was the first nationally distributed Christmas craft beer in America, for a brief period shortly after Prohibition, Miller Brewing Company also made a holiday lager.

Miller Special Christmas beer appeared in stores in 1935, with a label that showed a happy family enjoying a couple glasses by the fire. The beer quickly disappeared from production, however, and there's no one left at the brewery who remembers what it tasted like.

Dozens of regional beer makers—those who distributed within one hundred miles of their breweries—also got into the spirit around the same time.

In upstate New York, the Fred Koch Brewery produced cans and bottles of Koch's Holiday Beer—

possibly even prior to Prohibition. "My grandfather started the brewery in 1888, and when he passed away in 1911, his three sons—William, Fred, and Henry—ran it afterwards," says John Koch, the last family member to brew the brand. "The recipe [for the holiday beer] was passed on to my father and then to me. We just always did it." Koch remembers the beer as a slightly heavier, darker lager than Koch's usual beer. "People really looked forward to it, and it was a very, very successful thing for us because November and December are usually a slow season for a brewery." But the brand disappeared when Genesee took over Koch in the 1990s. Old-timers who long for Koch's Holiday Beer should try Koch's Golden Anniversary, now made by High Falls Brewing—it's virtually the same beer.

In Wisconsin, several small breweries produced Christmas beers beginning in the 1940s (and ending in the 1970s) that were distributed as far as Chicago. To this day, you can still find labels for holiday beers from Marathon City, Huber, Peoples, and Chief Oshkosh for sale on eBay. Close to the Mississippi River, the Potosi Brewing Company symbolically changed its name each year to the "Holiday Brewing Company" to produce its Wisconsin Holiday Beer in the 1940s.

In Bethlehem, Pennsylvania, officially dubbed America's Christmas City, a local brewery produced Heidelberg Holiday Beer in the 1940s. In Evanston, Wyoming, Becker's bottled an American pilsner called Xmas Brew around the same period .

And then there was Walter's Holiday Beer from Eau Claire, Wisconsin. The beer—a slightly hoppy, darker pilsner—debuted in 1954, as Tom Walter, the former brewmaster, recalls. "I came up with the idea of putting a smiley face on the crowns that said, 'Smile it's the holidays!'" Walter says. "They were different colors, so when you opened up the case, it was colorful, like Christmas decorations." The holiday beer sold so well, the company slapped a new label on the bottle during the summer months and sold it as Walter's Special Beer (production ended in the 1960s).

Visitors can see how a nineteenth-century beer baron enjoyed Christmas at the Pabst Mansion in Milwaukee. The Victorian house, once home to Captain Frederick Pabst, is lavishly decorated inside and out for the holidays. Tours run from Thanksgiving to mid-January. Unfortunately, they don't serve Pabst Blue Ribbon.

TIDINGS OF COMFORT
AND JULEØL

I n tiny Honningsvag, Norway, one of the northernmost towns in the world, on the day when the sun is at its lowest ebb, Hans Magne Olsen reenacts an age-old tradition: in darkness, he raises a glass of festive beer and toasts the winter solstice.

Olsen is the brewer at the Nordkapp Bryggeri, the world's northernmost brewpub. Located in an Arctic fishing village 1,311 miles from the North Pole, it is virtually the last place on earth where you can drink a fresh, handcrafted beer.

"I love the darkness," Olsen tells me during a visit while we sip his juleøl, Norway's traditional Christmas beer. "I feel more secure."

In the darkness, you understand why nowhere else in the world has a stronger Christmas beer tradition than Norway. In this cold country, every brewery produces two, three, or more different Christmas beers each season to help keep warm during the long winter nights. In a nation of fewer than four million adults, there are at least fifty different Christmas beers to choose from. Beer drinkers pack the state-run Vinmonopolet—the state alcohol monopoly—to collect and savor the varieties. The newspapers conduct serious judging panels to rate each; the champions sell out immediately.

Oddly, many of the beers are nearly identical—a malty amber brew that might be described as a light bock or a Vienna lager. The only thing special about the beer is the label.

That, and the tradition.

Juleøl (from *Jul*, meaning "winter feast," and *øl*, meaning "beer") is the world's oldest continually brewed Christmas beer. It has been made in Norway since well before the birth of Christ, when tribal sects celebrated the solstice with Jul feasts in honor of the gods Odin and Thor. To these early

Øl i skatteklasse 2 fra
Grans Bryggeri, Sandefjord
Etablert i 1899

dwellers, the longest night of the year marked the reemergence of the sun and the rebirth of the earth. It was a sign that the days would begin to lengthen, and that the earth would once again become fertile. With the autumn crops harvested, the animals slaughtered, and the beer fully fermented, villagers came together for days of feasting. It was a ritual affair, with many glasses raised to the gods, and to good fortune. The beer and the festival became inseparable.

"It was a time to charge your batteries for the harsh winter ahead," explains Torbjørn K. Skogvold, spokesman for the Aass brewery in Drammen, just south of Oslo. "People had a hard life. It was cold, they didn't have proper clothing, it was tough. But if you could drink well and eat well, you'd feel warm."

The festival and its beer became so institutionalized that by AD 800, Norwegian farmers were required by law to brew juleøl. "You had to make a beer with as much grain as the combined weight of the farm's husband and wife," Skogvold says. "And it had to be strong beer. If it wasn't, it was considered dishonorable and your farm would have a spell cast on it." Worse, if the farmer failed to make juleøl for three consecutive years, Skogvold says, his property could be seized, and he would be expelled from the country.

A Viking wouldn't say he celebrated Jul—he drank it, and drank lots. To stop drinking to anything less than a stupor was bad manners. When King Håkon I declared in AD 900 that Jul would be held on December 25 in honor of Christ, not the pagan gods, Norwegians didn't put down their goblets.

The ancient style of beer is still made today on tiny farms outside the western fjord town of Trondheim, in the Stjørdal region. First the farmers make their own malt, steeping it in large tubs for three days, and then drying it on boards over smoking fires made with alder wood. About thirty malt houses dot the surrounding landscape; when they are fired up, the farmers notify the local airport to make sure the smoke doesn't interfere with flights.

"I brew just like my father did," says Morten Granås, a seventy-year-old local farmer and woodworker who started making beer when he was fifteen. Looking at his spartan equipment—a tub to cook the malt, another to ferment the beer—you get the sense that little has changed in twenty generations.

Each year on December 9—the same day Norwegian housewives traditionally begin making their famous lutefisk (lye-soaked cod)—the farmers start to brew. Depending on their variety, they may add spices, juniper berries, or just a handful of fresh hops to the smoky malt. In the old days, it would have sat uncovered until fermentation began. These days, however, the brewers pitch in basic baker's yeast—although I've heard that some still keep the tradition of yelling loudly at the brew to "scare" it into bubbling. Within ten days, it's ready to be bottled. The choice of containers varies. For example, in his only concession to modern times, Granås uses empty plastic Pepsi bottles.

On the day after Christmas, the local farmers gather to sample one another's juleøl. The flavor is unlike that of any other beer in the world. It is deeply smoky (far smokier than Bamberg, Germany's famous rauchbier) and mildly spicy. It tastes a bit like munching on some smoked turkey, in a pine forest—a pine forest that happens to be on fire.

Since it's not for sale, even in Norway few people get to savor this special Christmas beer—or would even want to. For them, the standard commercial juleøl is enough of a reminder of the ancient winter solstice celebration.

Because any beer over 4.7 percent alcohol must be sold at the Vinmonopolet, most large brewers produce lower alcohol versions of their juleøl. Norwegian beer aficionados scoff at the stuff, and instead scour the Internet for lists of available strong—or *sterkøl*—juleøl.

Several Norwegian microbreweries have cropped up in recent years to meet the demand. Notable among these is Nøgne Ø, which makes God Jul, and Haandbryggeriet, which makes Nissemor. Both are exported to the United States.

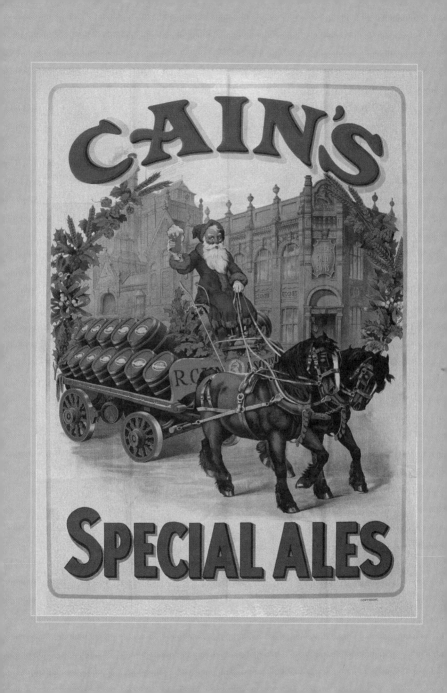

JOY TO THE WORLD

While the joyful spirit of giving is universal, the celebration of Christmas differs from country to country. Some cultures follow centuries-old folk traditions, whereas others—thanks to immigration and globalization—have adopted traditions from foreign lands.

More often than not, however, the occasion is marked with a special beer.

Australia/New Zealand

Christmas arrives in early summer in the southern hemisphere, so instead of hot cocoa, Santa (who rides on a sleigh pulled by six white kangaroos) gets a cold beer. Often, families celebrate the holiday with a cold ham dinner or seafood on a local beach.

Austria

Families might sing a few verses of "Stille Nacht" (Silent Night), which was written in the region of Salzburg. For dinner, they enjoy *Gebackener Karpfen*—braised carp, served with gingerbread in a beer sauce.

Belgium

Watch out for Père Fouettard (the Whipping Father), the dark figure that accompanies St. Nicolas in French-speaking Belgium. After their visit from him, Belgians traditionally drink an extra-strong Scottish ale. However, this style of beer is disappearing, as the nation's many breweries instead produce sweeter, abbey-style beers for the holidays.

Britain

After the turkey and stuffing comes a classic Christmas dessert: plum pudding. This lavish dish is made with dried fruits, nuts, and suet that is cooked and stirred for hours. It's often prepared and dried out for a few weeks before the holiday feast, when it is served with sugar and may be moistened with an ample dousing of black stout.

Denmark

Danes begin celebrating the holiday on the first Friday of November, known as J-Dag—the day their beloved *julebryg*, or Christmas beer, is released. The larger breweries, including Tuborg and Carlsberg, make a big deal out of the event, sending out horse-drawn wagons at exactly 8:59 p.m. to deliver the first batch.

On Christmas Eve, mugs of steaming *gløgg*—a drink made with raisins, almonds, spices, and aquavit—are served while families exchange presents. Children often drink a sweetened, low-alcohol variety of *Jule brug* (Yule brew).

Estonia

In the old days, farmers brewed a Christmas beer on St. Thomas Day, December 21. It was a quick and easy beer to make that would be drained by New Year's Day.

Today St. Thomas Day marks the start of the holiday feasting, which features plates of blood pudding, sausage, pork, and sauerkraut. Here they favor sweet beer to wash down ginger-snaps and *piparkoogid*, cookies made with peppercorns, cocoa, and cinnamon.

Finland

Before Santa visits, even kids drink *jouluolut*, homemade Christmas beer still found in many homes in Finland. It's a sugary, low-alcohol drink made with powdered rye malt, flour, and sugar. No hops are added, and it only takes a week to ferment.

Glasses of the sweet stuff share a place at the dinner table with reindeer meat, lutefisk (dried cod soaked in lye), and *karjalanpaisti*, a hot pot made with pork and beef.

France

Christmas is called Noël, and it's celebrated on the night before with a lengthy dinner known as *réveillon*. The menu consists of gourmet dishes, like foie gras, oysters, and escargot, typically washed down not with beer, sadly, but with Champagne.

Germany

In many towns, craftsmen and shopkeepers set up lavish *Christkindlmarkts* (holiday markets) selling handmade decorations, puppets, toys, and wood carvings. It's a tradition to drink *glühwein*, a hot mulled wine, but usually you'll find a vendor selling bottles of *weihnachtsbier*—typically a bock.

On Christmas Eve, some traditionalists still serve *bier fisch*—carp cooked in beer.

Iceland

Thirteen mischievous *Jólasveinar*, or Yule Lads, traditionally pay a visit to households during the holiday season. At one time, the imps—with names like *Kleinusnikir* (Donut Beggar) and *Faldafeykir* (Skirt Blower)—were feared, but today they leave small gifts for the kids.

The traditional Þorrablót (Yule feast) predates Christmas and typically features old-fashioned dishes, including shark, salmon, and (ugh) sheep testicles. You'll want to wash that down, quickly, with a shot of *brennivin* (also commonly known as Black Death) and a Jolabjor chaser.

Ireland

After the kids hang their pillowcases (not stockings) by the chimney or at the foot of their beds, they leave mince pies, cookies, and a nice bottle of Guinness for Santa.

Italy

After mass, the famous Feast of the Seven Fishes is the highlight of Christmas Eve. Every family does it differently, but typically the dishes include *baccalà* (salt cod), calamari (squid), one whole fish such as tuna or sea bass, and, of course, pasta.

In the glasses? Usually it's a red table wine, but increasingly Italy is discovering hearty, full-flavored Belgian-style ales.

Latvia

What do you drink to wash down a traditional plate of boiled peas and fried meat? On Christmas Day, you might go for a glass of *r gušpiens* (curdled milk). Some places still celebrate *Ziemassvetki*, a winter festival in which townspeople gather around a bonfire and drink a honey beer called medalus.

Lithuania

During the traditional twelve-dish supper on Christmas Eve, hay is spread across the table to signify Christ's birth in the manger. Then a glass of beer or *kvass* (a type of beer made from black bread) is set on the table to mark the place of any recently deceased family members.

Luxembourg

St. Nicholas Day is the big day here, marked with a visit by Kleeschen and his dark sidekick, Hoùseker. Christmas Day is typically celebrated with large family dinners, often featuring black pudding with mashed potatoes and applesauce.

Mexico

Noche Buena (Holy Night) is the name of the country's only Christmas beer. Take a look at the label and you'll find a poinsettia, the colorful Christmas flower known as *la flor de Noche Buena* that is indigenous to Mexico.

The beer (and the flower) makes a festive accompaniment to overflowing bowls of *ensalada de Noche Buena* (Christmas Eve Salad) made with fruit, beets, jicama, and peanuts.

The Netherlands

Sinterklaas—the direct ancestor of America's Santa Claus—makes his appearance on the eve of St. Nicholas Day, December 5, along with his sidekick, Zwarte Piet (Black Peter).

Dutch beer drinkers get an early start on the holidays with the annual Bokbierfestival held in Amsterdam in autumn. It signals the start of strong beer season, with nearly every brewery producing a holiday brew called *kerstbier*.

Russia

The Russian Orthodox Church marks Christmas on January 7, the date of Christ's birth on the Julian calendar. Banned after the 1917 Revolution, the holiday was marked in subdued celebrations until 1992.

Today there's an old-world feel to the holiday, with all-night masses and rustic dinners that often include borscht made with home-brewed kvass.

Scotland

Hogmanay is the last day of the year, an event surely worth celebrating. It stretches from December 31 (Old Year's Night) to January 1 (Ne'er Day), and sometimes till January 2. Friends and family share a custom called "first-footing," in which the first person over one's threshold is expected to bring a gift of sweets and drinks.

And, if they're lucky, the host will serve them Clootie Dumpling, a boiled treat made with breadcrumbs, dried fruit, sugar, spice, and the magic ingredient: suet.

Sweden

Imagine an imperial stout for kids. That's julmust, a nonalcoholic Christmas drink made with sugar, hops, malt extract, and spices. It's dark and rich and exceptionally sweet—just the thing to get the kiddies pumped up while they're waiting to sit on Santa's lap. (In America, you can buy it at the Ikea furniture stores.)

For Christmas dinner, the smorgasbord is loaded with traditional pickled, smoked, salted, and dried fish, and topped off with mugs of glögg (hot mulled wine).

Switzerland

If you make your way to the Alpine village of Küssnacht, you'll find one of the oddest Christmas traditions around: *Klausjagen*, the great Santa Claus chase. On December 5, the eve of St. Nicholas Day, hundreds of townsfolk (men only) parade through the village cracking whips, ringing cowbells, blowing trumpets, and wearing elaborate paper hats as high as six feet lit beneath by candles. They're hunting for Santa Claus.

It goes without saying that a great deal of beer is consumed on this night, as taverns pass out free liters to costumed revelers.

OY! HOLY NIGHT

Hanukkah is not, contrary to some popular perceptions, the Jewish Christmas. There's no holy birth, no mythical gift giver, no flying animals. It is, in fact, a fairly minor holiday in Judaism.

However, that does not mean Hanukkah shouldn't have its own beer.

Behold: He'brew Jewbelation from Shmaltz Brewing.

And, no, this isn't some weak-flavored lager from the Festival of the Lights. It's one of the best holiday ales—whether for Christmas, Kwanzaa, Festivus, whatever—that you'll find at your local beer store, made by the same folks who bring you He'brew, the Chosen Beer.

Jewbelation is a massive, seriously made beer whose recipe changes annually. In its twelve years, each version has contained successively more and more hops. In 2007, its eleventh year, the ale was made with eleven different malts and eleven different hops, and contained 11 percent alcohol.

As soon as it shows up in stores, before Halloween, it begins turning heads—not an easy task when up against so many other, extraordinary holiday beers. *Celebrator*, the highly respected West Coast beer trade paper, once gave it a top rating of five stars. In 2006, *Pacific Brew News* named it best of show in a blind tasting of more than thirty wintertime beers, ahead of the likes of Anderson Valley Winter Solstice and the near-mythic Alaskan Smoked Porter. "I think it is safe to say this was a surprise for most of us," the newspaper acknowledged, "but this beer had it all."

"It's fantastic," says Jeremy Cowan, the man behind the beer. "This kind of response is exactly the goal I had in mind with He'brew. People are starting to take the beer really seriously." Which, admittedly, is a bit difficult when you plow through all of Cowan's hilarious Jewish hype ("The first ever extreme high holiday beer") and a wordy press package that attempts to explain the meaning behind each year's number.

Dark brown with a tan head, the most recent version of Jewbelation explodes with a malty aroma right out of the bottle. The hops don't jump out of the glass, but instead mellow that sweet flavor and disguise its very powerful kick.

Yes, with double-digit alcohol percentage, a 22-ounce bomber will have you on your knees, and not necessarily out of religious devotion. "This Hanukkah," Cowen quips, "the candles won't be the only thing getting lit."

L'chaim!

Most beer is regarded as kosher because its raw ingredients (barley, hops, and water) do not violate the *kashruth*, or Jewish dietary laws. The only concerns arise in beers with flavoring additives or specialty yeasts, like those used in barleywine. The Chicago Rabbinical Council says all nonflavored U.S. beers, including dark beer, are kosher.

Kwanzaa Beer

So far, nobody has made a commercial ale to toast the Pan-African festival of Kwanzaa. But it is traditional to drink ginger beer for the celebration. Here's an easy recipe.

- 5 ounces ginger
- 2 ounces honey
- 2 ounces lime juice
- 2 quarts water
- 1 egg white, beaten
- 3 cups sugar
- ¼ ounce dry yeast

Mince or pound ginger. Mix into a sauce pan with honey, lime, sugar, and water, heat to a lukewarm temperature (about 100 degrees). Turn off heat; let cool for 30 minutes. Strain into a gallon jug.

Mix yeast into beaten egg white. Add mixture to the jug and shake lightly.

Cap the jug tightly and let it sit in a cool place. When it stops bubbling (usually in a week), it's ready to drink.

HO, HO, HIC!

With his red nose, bulging belly, and hearty laugh, Santa Claus looks like the original party animal. Brewing companies couldn't ask for a better celebrity endorsement.

At holiday time, he can be seen raising a glass of George Gale's Christmas Ale or giving the thumbs up to Butte Creek Christmas Cranberry. On ceramic bottles of Delirium Noël, he drives a sleigh led by tiny pink elephants. And he's been selling beer for years. In the 1930s, Goebel Beer urged customers to "drink deep of the brew that restores one's faith in Santa Claus." Forget jolly—some breweries portrayed the elf as completely soused.

But should Santa really be shilling for suds?

This question crops up every few years, usually from parents who complain that this symbol of childhood innocence should be protected from Madison Avenue. Never mind that Claus poetically arrives with such a clatter that Mama in her kerchief doesn't much appreciate some old guy belching, "Whazzup!"

The irony is that Santa has always been a shill—for Coca Cola, Macy's, Jello, you name it. Almost immediately after cartoonist Thomas Nast inked the first popular illustration of Kris Kringle in 1863, advertisers used the image to sell products, and nothing was off-limits. Forget about those quaint visions of sugarplums dancing in your head—by 1901, jolly old St. Nick was already showing up in newspaper ads with a stogie stuck in his mouth, proudly commending the merits of New Brunswick ten-cent cigars. A few years later, a full-color *Life* magazine ad portrayed a soused Santa reading kiddies' letters while sucking down a bottle of whiskey.

Prohibition was a mere sabbatical for America's bearded beer man. As soon as the Eighteenth Amendment was repealed in December 1933 (just in time for Christmas!), he was back caging for breweries. "Join Mr. Claus (who has a fond regard for the best things in life) in drinking tangy, foamy, and delicious Point Special," one ad urged.

CHRISTMAS COMES BUT ONCE A YEAR........

But you can get CENTLIVRE Beer, just about the best beer on earth, all the year 'round. Spring, Summer, Autumn and Winter—it's always refreshing, palatable, ..appetite-bringing nourishing, because it's made from the purest materials, by the cleanest methods, by skilled brewers. Make Santa Claus your servitor and bring good cheer in the shape of CENTLIVRE Beer into your home.

The waning Temperance movement was not amused. Still hoping for a return to Prohibition, its supporters tried to rally the troops with Santa Claus. In 1936, Ethel Hubler, a popular radio talk show host and head of the Los Angeles chapter of the Women's Christian Temperance Union (WCTU), campaigned to outlaw the use of Santa in booze ads. "Last year," Hubler complained to Congress, "Santa Claus, patron saint of children during the holiday season, was pictured loaded down with beer bottles, drinking cocktails, serving as bartender, and in similar roles." Instead of shrugging off the gripe as sour grapes from sore losers, lawmakers across the country caved in to the WCTU. Eventually, at least thirty states enacted laws banning Santa from beer ads. "The attitude of this board," ruled the head of the District of Columbia's alcohol agency, "is definitely against any advertising copy which links liquor to the Bible, or which pictures Santa Claus dealing or carrying . . . alcoholic beverages." A 1936 *Time* magazine report noted that only fun-loving New York declined to pass any laws to protect Santa. "Authorities declared that the patron of Christmas is 'not actually a saint, but a character of fiction, not a biblical character, but merely the symbol of happiness and good cheer.'"

Most beer companies backed off, switching to wreaths and holly and wholesome images of cheerful adults sharing sixpacks 'neath the mistletoe. The notable exception was Anheuser-Busch. For half a century, Santa appeared prominently in its ads, declaring that Budweiser was as much a part of Christmas as jingle bells and eggnog. Look closely at one ad from the 1940s, and you'll see the red-suited elf in a sleigh full of kegs and cases, pulled by a team of Clydesdales. It wasn't until 1987 that the beer giant got its wrists slapped. That year, Anheuser-Busch decorated cases of Bud Light with its famous spokesdog, Spuds MacKenzie, dressed in a red Santa suit. Officials in

Utah and Ohio barked that the merchandising violated bans on depicting Santa in liquor ads and ordered the cases removed.

It's not only conservative U.S. states that have acted to protect Santa's honor. In 1997, authorities in Canada ordered a tiny Montreal brewery called Brasseurs GMT to yank five thousand cases of its Bière de Noël from store shelves simply because the bottles carried a drawing of Santa.

Usually, government authorities win these cases: after all, they make the rules. But recently, a small specialty importer from Massachusetts fought back—and won. The company, Shelton Brothers, markets a set of Christmas beers from Ridgeway Brewing in England with names like Santa's Butt Winter Porter and Very Bad Elf Special Reserve Ale. The labels typically depict Santa or his wayward elves in some compromised position. In 2005 and 2006, authorities in Connecticut, Maine, and New York sought to ban sales of the brews, claiming they violated their protectionist Santa standards. The labels, they said, might entice a minor to drink—a laughable argument considering the expense (about five dollars a bottle) of the imported ales. Maine said it was "undignified and improper" to depict Santa dangling precariously over an open fire on the label of Warm Welcome Nut Browned Ale. Connecticut placed Mr. Claus in the company of holy saints, saying its alcohol regulations outlaw the use of his image, or anyone from the Bible, in liquor ads. (Mother's Day beer ads are a no-no, too.)

In 1939, the state of California attempted to ban the use of Santa Claus's image in advertising of any kind. "Santa Claus primarily belongs to the children," Senator Harry C. Westover of Santa Ana declared in the New York Times.

Using Santa in advertising and marketing materials, by the way, is a violation of the Beer Institute's own ethical guidelines. But when the Bad Elf case cropped up, the lobby group's president, Jeff Becker, instead defended the Sheltons' right to singe Santa's behind. The institute's guidelines are merely "voluntary," he notes. Government agencies should butt out "because of the First Amendment."

Facing costly sales bans, the Sheltons turned to the American Civil Liberties Union (ACLU) for help, and, suddenly, Santa found himself in the middle of a constitutional battle. During one liquor board hearing, an ACLU attorney argued that the law was a violation of the First Amendment's establishment clause, which restricts the government's preference of one religion over another.

Eventually, a constitutional crisis was averted. All three states backed off, lamely rationalizing that their Santa regulations didn't apply to labels.

So the question remains: should Santa be shilling for suds?

In a letter to the Shelton Brothers, one Methodist minister typified the position of Santa fundamentalists: "This is a positive image of our culture and an image that children love. To put Santa on a beer can is just disgusting. If your beer cannot sell itself without exploiting the Santa Claus image, then it must not be very good beer. . . . Please reconsider your use of Santa. Think of the children!"

Dan Shelton replied, "Giving Santa Claus the boot obviously won't do anything to curb underage drinking. As we all know, there's a ton of advertising out in the market playing on themes like partying and sex that's infinitely more appealing to minors—and adults—than Santa will ever be. . . . It's hard to avoid the suspicion that picking on Santa is just an easy way to appear to be doing something about the problem without actually doing something about it."

About 40 percent of men over age thirty in the United Kingdom say that if they were Santa for one night, they'd prefer it if kids left them a pint of beer with those cookies.

SANTA LIVES

Yes, Virginia, there is a Santa Claus beer.

It exists as certainly as love and generosity and devotion exist. It is dark and strong and full of good cheer. And it is born each year on December 6, St. Nicholas Day, inside the stainless-steel vats of Schloss Eggenberg brewery at the foot of the Alps in western Austria.

It is Samichlaus, the world's most famous Christmas beer.

Brewed just one day a year, the lager sits in those vats for ten months, before being bottled and delivered the following Christmas season to a waiting world of beer lovers. It is so cherished that a local priest offers a blessing in the brewery's chapel as the bubbling batch is brewed.

Indeed, it took a miracle—and even some faith on the part of beer aficionados—for this beer to even exist.

Since its beginning almost thirty years ago, Samichlaus has been a cult favorite, partly because of its distinct flavor, but also thanks to its resounding strength. It is 14 percent alcohol—more potent even than most wine. In 1990, the *Guinness Book of Records* named it the Strongest Lager in the World. (Other beers, like Samuel Adams Triple Bock, have more alcohol, but they are made with a variety of ale, lager, and Champagne yeast strains, so they are not considered authentic lagers.)

Disaster struck in the late 1990s, though, when Hürlimann, the Swiss brewery that had made the beer since 1980, was bought by the Feldschlösschen brewing combine. With little respect for this niche product, the heartless conglomerate quietly killed Santa . . . uh, I mean, Samichlaus.

An international campaign to save the brand was launched. Petitions were signed. Beer fans wrote letters. Famed beer writer Michael Jackson, who had declared the beer "a world classic," urged the brewery to reconsider.

It remained gone for a year or two, but then—in a stroke of good fortune—Schloss Eggenberg stepped in. Under an unusual licensing agreement, the brewery brought Samichlaus back, using the same ingredients, the same recipe, even the same secret yeast as the original.

While Samichlaus is ready for drinking once it's bottled, the strong lager reveals itself more intimately after years of cellaring. Does the recipe change from year to year, or is it the natural result of maturation? Even the folks at Eggenberg are unsure.

More recent bottles tend to be full of malt flavor. Wait a year, and the fruitier esters emerge and remind you of peach brandy. Wait three or four years, and the lager becomes even more delicate, its edges smoothed over with time. I've tasted bottles that were ten years old and more and found that what started out as a loud, head-banging lager had finally settled down and allowed me to see its softer side.

Built on the site of a tenth-century castle (*schloss* in German), Eggenberg is an oddity among Austrian breweries. While most produce standard pilsners and mildly malty lagers served in frothy half-liter mugs, this small brewery decided that if it was going to survive, it would have to develop its export products. "There was no chance to compete against the big groups," says Karl Stöhr, the managing director of Eggenberg International whose family has owned the brewery since 1803. "We knew that we had to do something special." Like creating Urbock, its famously strong (9.6 percent alcohol) bock that is now distributed in thirty-five countries, and Nessie, a hearty whiskey-malt beer.

Though these big beers have garnered international praise, they are hardly known in Austria. Stöhr says this is due to the Austrian mentality. "They're conservative; they're not used to drinking strong beer. They drink a lot of the traditional beer, but they don't have any idea that the world of beer is bigger than lager and pils. . . . It's not like America, where people are open to more different tastes."

Eggenberg, built on a site where beer has been brewed since the 1300s, treats Samichlaus with utter reverence. On brewing day, it invites a handful

of clients and journalists to attend the ceremonial tasting of the wort—the warm, malty unfermented liquid that is the basis of all beer. A local priest says a blessing. Then tall pilsner glasses of the murky porridge are poured directly from a huge copper lauter tun. It looks threatening, like a witch's brew, but it goes down like a mouth-warming mulled cider, thick and sticky and sweet.

How sweet?

In Europe, brewers use the Plato scale to measure original gravity—the amount of sugar dissolved in water. More sugar, of course, means more alcohol upon fermentation. Samichlaus measures about 27–30 on the scale, compared to 16–17 for a typical bock. To measure this in the old days, before hydrometers were used, recalls Eggenberg brewer Anton Hemetsberger with a sly smile, you'd pour some of the freshly boiled wort onto a small wooden bench and sit on it. If the bench stuck to your butt when you stood up, Hemetsberger continues, it was a bock. Presumably, if you poured some Samichlaus, you could get a La-Z-Boy to stick to your seat.

Of course, the secret of Samichlaus is deeper than that sticky solution. Anyone can dissolve sugar in water; the trick is converting it into drinkable alcohol. The secret—the stuff that makes this the world's strongest lager—is the yeast.

If you watched Hemetsberger as he works the cooled brew, you wouldn't notice anything different from any of the other batches. He pitches the same house yeast used in all the Eggenberg brands. The yeast bravely churns through the sugar until it peters out at about 10 percent alcohol.

That's when the brewmaster turns to a second batch of yeast, a wondrous mix unlike anything else in his brewery. This is an uberyeast propagated from a strain that was isolated years ago by Hürlimann, a yeast that can continue its metabolic mission into the highest alcoholic realm.

Any brewer will tell you that secondary fermentation is a difficult, touchy task. Pushing alcohol to 14 percent is craft and science and a little intuition. "It's like with your wife," says Hemetsberger. "You have to know where to touch to get the right result."

It takes about ten to twelve more days for the bubbling brew to reach that lofty 14 percent level. Ten months of aging in cool cellar vats follow, until it's ready for the next holiday season. The result is a true triple bock—no adjuncts, no maple syrup—made with nothing more than malt, water, hops, yeast, and a lot of faith.

No Samichlaus? Thank God, Samichlaus lives on. A thousand years from now, Virginia, nay, ten times ten thousand years from now, it will continue to make glad the heart of all lovers of beer.

In 2007, Schloss Eggenberg revived the production of Samichlaus Helles, a pale version of traditional Samichlaus that is golden and translucent, but just as strong at 14 percent alcohol.

O, LITTLE TOWN OF
BETHLEHEM, PENNSYLVANIA

Rudolph the red-nosed reindeer had a very shiny nose . . . and a good lawyer.

And if you have any doubt, consider what happened in Bethlehem, the eastern Pennsylvania steel town named for the biblical birthplace of Christ.

In 2003, Bethlehem Brew Works brewed up a batch of holiday ale. It was deep red, spiced with cinnamon and nutmeg, and it jingled your bells at a jolly old 9.5 percent alcohol. As brewer Jeff Fegley says, "When you smell the beer, you think Christmas."

The ale, like all those at the brewpub, had been available only on draft. But the family-run pub figured the Christmas beer would be perfect to launch its new line of bottled brews because, as Fegley says, "Bethlehem is 'the Christmas City.'" The brewpub took its recipe to a nearby production brewery, cooked up a batch, and proceeded to bottle the ale. All they needed was a name for the label.

Originally, they'd called it plain Christmas Ale. But they wanted something snappier, so they held a name-the-beer contest. It received hundreds of entries, and the winner got dinner and a free supply of the special ale.

The winning name: Rudolph's Reserve.

Looking back on it now, Fegley says, "We could've probably gotten away with it if it weren't for the label." Ah yes, the label. It's a witty caricature by Maryland artist Robert C. Matteson, depicting St. Nick pulling a bottle from Rudolph's saddlebag. Poor Rudolph, he looked a bit spooked by Santa's claws.

It wasn't long until Rudolph's lawyer put an end to the fun.

In a dispute that's not unusual in the beer business, the brewpub found itself slapped with one of those tough-sounding "cease and desist" letters intended to shake the tinsel off your tree. An attorney identifying himself as a representative of the Rudolph Company said Bethlehem had infringed on its trademark.

Rudolph the red-nosed reindeer, a registered trademark?

As it turns out, Rudolph was created in 1939 by an advertising copywriter at the old Montgomery Ward department store in Chicago. The writer, Robert L. May, came up with Rudolph and his nose for a Christmastime promotional booklet. His daughter, Virginia Herz, told me: "Most people think Rudolph and Santa have been together forever. My father's story was an amazing contribution to the lore of Christmas."

Herz says that in 1946 Montgomery Ward reverted Rudolph's trademark rights to her father. Three years later, May's brother-in-law, songwriter Johnny Marks, penned the familiar holiday tune. The song became a huge holiday hit after it was recorded by cowboy singer Gene Autry, selling more than thirty million copies. It became a permanent part of American culture when Burl Ives narrated the famously kitschy 1964 animated television special *Rudolph the Red-Nosed Reindeer*. More than sixty years after the cute, four-legged creature was invented, Rudolph lives on in countless decorations, books, and dozens of modern song versions, from folk to rap.

May died in 1976, but his family retained rights to the image through the Rudolph Company, whose lawyer keeps busy firing off cease-and-desist letters every time he comes across anyone using the name to sell something without permission. Fegley's letter was a classic bit of lawyer-ese. It said the brewery would have to remove any image of "a red-tipped nose on any deer-like animal." Adds Fegley: "Our lawyer mentioned that they had even gone after someone who had a picture of a cow with a red nose and antlers, and pressured them out of using the image. It was depicting an image that was degrading the Rudolph image."

It's not hard to understand why the trademark owners would be touchy. Rudolph is foremost a kids' favorite, not a Spuds MacKenzie beer shill.

Of course, there is that famous crimson honker, a bulbous shiner that puts W.C. Fields's schnozz to shame. But when I mentioned this to Herz, she recoiled: "The red nose was never meant to be associated with inebriation."

As for Bethlehem's version, Fegley notes, "There wasn't any rude or crude use of the name. It wasn't like we were depicting a drunken Rudolph stumbling. It was a bit frustrating." But he acknowledges: "I kind of understand. When you have a trademark, you have to go after everyone that has some likeness."

Bethlehem might have received permission to use it if it had paid a royalty. Instead, it backed down and agreed to stop using the name. The 2003 batch of five hundred cases became a collector's item; the next year, the beer had a new name and label. "It's not a do-or-die situation for us," Fegley says. "We're just a brewpub. It's not worth it to us to fight."

Maybe not, but the brewery seemingly got in the last word on this yuletide battle. The next year, it came up with a new bottle for its holiday ale. Look closely at the label, and you'll see that the Christmas elf seems to be flipping the bird. At whom? Perhaps Rudolph's lawyer.

And the new name?

Rude Elf's Reserve.

Rude Elf's Reserve is one of those highly spiced brews that makes you think you're drinking Red Zinger tea with a kick. The ale, backed by three different Belgian yeasts, comes through nicely, though, for a festive holiday flavor. Fegley suggests letting the bottle warm up to about 50 degrees. Then sip it beside a fire, maybe on one foggy Christmas Eve.

The World's 50 Best
CHRISTMAS BEERS

1.   Mad Elf

Tröegs Brewing
Harrisburg, Pennsylvania
www.troegs.com
Style: **BELGIAN STRONG DARK ALE**
Alcohol volume: 11%
Serve with: Bacon quiche, blue cheese with pears

Brothers John and Chris Trogner are reluctant to call this ruby-colored gem a Belgian-style ale, but that's only because it's almost unclassifiable. Though it's brewed with honey and tart Pennsylvania cherries, the dominant character here is a ginger and clove spiciness, a product of its unique pair of Belgian yeast strains. Think fruitcake, but not the awful one made by your Aunt Bertha. This beer tastes like it's been aged in an apple cider cask. You'll find it on draft and in bottles in the Northeast, but you've got to be quick—it sells out every year. The ultimate Mad Elf is the corked and boxed 101-ounce jeroboam, ideal for long-term cellaring or bringing to a holiday party. Whether in a small bottle or a large one, however, it's worth saving in your cellar to enjoy in later years. The spice mellows nicely, leaving a deeply satisfying winelike flavor. It's a fine example of how American microbrewers have taken old-world styles and created an entirely new—and ultimately superb—Christmas beer.

❄ • ❄ • ❄ • ❄ • ❄ • ❄ • ❄ • ❄ • ❄ • ❄ • ❄ • ❄ • ❄ • ❄ • ❄ • ❄ • ❄ • ❄

Each summer, Tröegs kegs a second version called Naked Elf that is made from the same recipe as Mad Elf, only without the cherries.

2. Avec les Bons Voeux

La Brasserie Dupont
Tourpes, Belgium
No Web site
Style: **SAISON**
Alcohol volume: 9.5%
Serve with: Braised veal shanks

La Brasserie Dupont is like much of Wallonia, the French-speaking region of Belgium: quiet, hardworking, idyllic in a nostalgic way. It is still a farm, with a fromagerie and boulangerie on the premises. Not much has changed since it began brewing in 1844, making a traditional ale known as saison—French for "season," referring to summer months when the ale would slowly ferment in cool cellars, to be opened for the thirsty farm workers at harvest time. Murky with suspended yeast, Dupont's well-known saison is regarded by many experts as one of the finest beers in the world. Imagine, then, taking that beer and making it even more special. Avec les Bon Voeux means "with our best wishes," and the bottle was originally intended as a gift to the brewery's workers—but one that was too good to be kept out of the hands of adoring Dupont fans. Uncork a bottle, and you're met with the delicate perfumelike aroma of hops. It refreshes from the first sip, but slow down, enjoy it with dinner and discover layer upon layer of flavor, including pepper, lemon, and clove. There are no spices here, however. That's just the natural flavor of tradition.

❅ • ❅ • ❅ • ❅ • ❅ • ❅ • ❅ • ❅ • ❅ • ❅ • ❅ • ❅ • ❅ • ❅ • ❅ • ❅ • ❅ • ❅ • ❅

In the mid-1990s, beer critic Michael Jackson called saison an "endangered species." Since then, American craft brewers—notably New York's Southampton and Ommegang breweries—have championed the style and spurred its resurgence.

3. Samichlaus Bier

Schloss Eggenberg
Vorchdorf, Austria
www.schloss-eggenberg.at
Style: **TRIPLE BOCK**
Alcohol volume: 14%
Serve with: Venison, brownie torte, chocolate truffles

On St. Nicholas Day in Switzerland, naughty children are warned, "Be good or Schmutzli will carry you off in his bag!" Dark and intimidating, Schmutzli is the sooty companion to the more likable Samichlaus, the Swiss-German name for Santa Claus. But when it comes to beer, it's Samichlaus who's the intimidator. Fourteen percent alcohol? That's no misprint: it's three times as strong as the average beer. Let it warm up in a snifter, and you'll think you're sipping brandy. It's best when shared in front of a fireplace while waiting for a visit from St. Nick. Or Schmutzli.

Samichlaus almost disappeared in the late nineties, when its Swiss brewer was bought by a conglomerate that thought the niche beer was unprofitable. After an international campaign was launched to save the brew, Austria's Schloss Eggenberg brewery took over its production.

4. Stille Nacht

Brouwerij De Dolle Brouwers
Essen, Belgium
www.dedollebrouwers.be
Style: **BELGIAN STRONG PALE ALE**
Alcohol volume: 12%
Serve with: A slab of ripe Limburger cheese

You don't have to be fluent in Dutch to understand that this beer means "Silent Night." Polish off just one bottle and it's sweet dreams, baby Jesus. The secret is pounds of candy sugar, a classic Belgian brewing trick that helps pump up the alcohol. Apples are also in there, but you'd be hard pressed to taste them. It might be my imagination, but this ale seems to have gotten sweeter in recent years—almost like a dessert wine. While De Dolle Brouwers (The Mad Brewers) produces only an exceedingly small amount of this ale, a surprisingly good percentage makes its way to the United States. The brewers urge you to age bottles for a decade or longer, but why wait? Head over to Antwerp, where the famous Kulminator tavern pours carefully cellared ten-year-old bottles into the proper glassware.

❅•❅•❅•❅•❅•❅•❅•❅•❅•❅•❅•❅•❅•❅•❅•❅•❅•❅•❅

A celebrated version of Stille Nacht, called Special Reserva, is matured for eighteen months in Bordeaux wine casks and bottled in limited numbers.

5. Our Special Ale

Anchor Brewing

San Francisco, California

www.anchorbrewing.com

Style: **SPICED WINTER WARMER**

Alcohol volume: Varies, about 5.5%

Serve with: Gingersnaps, cranberry salad

In 1975, Anchor launched an entire brewing tradition with this ale, the first true Christmas beer to be distributed across America since Prohibition. The label changes every year, with a drawing of a different featured tree. The recipe changes, too, causing fans to go on a mad spree to identify its spices. Flavors of chestnut, evergreen, licorice, nutmeg, ginger, and pumpkin have been among those detected. Sometimes there is even a whiff of cooked fruit. Lately, the beer has been somewhat bitter, but brewer Fritz Maytag won't even disclose the variety of hops in his famous beer. People keep guessing, though, taking stabs on beer appreciation blogs and even storing bottles from year to year, hoping to detect slight changes in flavor. I find the spices begin to fade by the time the summer arrives, so drink up and don't ask questions.

❄ • ❄ • ❄ • ❄ • ❄ • ❄ • ❄ • ❄ • ❄ • ❄ • ❄ • ❄ • ❄ • ❄ • ❄ • ❄ • ❄ • ❄

The first bottles of Our Special Ale didn't have printed neck labels, so Fritz and his kids simply signed the bottles with a pen, "Merry Christmas from the Maytags."

6. Celebration Ale

Sierra Nevada
Chico, California
www.sierranevada.com
Style: **INDIA PALE ALE**
Alcohol volume: 6.8%
Serve with: Leftover curried turkey sandwiches

Forget that first flurry in November, this snowy label is the true first sign of the start of the winter season, usually appearing on shelves just after Halloween. Sierra Nevada was founded by a home brewer who learned that the quality of ingredients—especially hops—was paramount in producing great flavor. Introduced in the early eighties, this mouthwatering bitter ale stunned beer freaks with its extraordinary Cascades and Centennial hops aroma. One restaurant critic (possibly after consuming a sixpack or two) emphatically declared it "the best beer ever made in America." Over the years other American brewers have caught up, and what was once regarded as an "extreme" or excessively hopped beer has now become more commonplace—the sort of beer you might even enjoy in the middle of July. Still, this rich ale is perfectly balanced and, for many, it wouldn't be the holidays without Celebration Ale.

❧ · ❧ · ❧ · ❧ · ❧ · ❧ · ❧ · ❧ · ❧ · ❧ · ❧ · ❧ · ❧ · ❧ · ❧ · ❧ · ❧ · ❧

*Like many Sierra Nevada products, Celebration Ale is bottle conditioned: live yeast
and an extra dose of malt are added just before bottling, to promote a second fermentation
that produces carbonation in the bottle.*

7. Samuel Smith's Winter Welcome Ale

Samuel Smith Old Brewery
Tadcaster, England
No Web site
Style: **WINTER WARMER**
Alcohol volume: 6%
Serve with: Roasted turkey

Thirty years ago, winter warmer—the malty British wassail ale with hints of spice—was almost dead. There was perhaps only one brewery—Young's of London—that still made the style, and it received only a passing mention in British beer critic Michael Jackson's 1977 landmark *World Guide to Beer*. Thankfully, a Seattle wine importer named Charles Finkel read the book and, in a fateful stroke of good fortune, gave up the grape and embarked upon bringing Jackson's favorite beer styles to America. Finkel arranged for Yorkshire's Samuel Smith brewery to replicate a variety of nearly extinct English beers—oatmeal stout, nut brown ale, and, for the holidays, winter warmer. He designed the handsome label and charged a then-unheard-of ten dollars per sixpack, and beer fans happily shelled out the dough. Other British brewers went back to their recipe books and reintroduced their own versions, and then American microbrewers tweaked the ingredients. By the late nineties, winter warmer was the world's most popular seasonal beer. This joyously rich, creamy, malty wonder is still the benchmark.

❅ • ❅ • ❅ • ❅ • ❅ • ❅ • ❅ • ❅ • ❅ • ❅ • ❅ • ❅ • ❅ • ❅ • ❅ • ❅ • ❅ • ❅ • ❅

Says importer Charles Finkel: "If Michael Jackson hadn't written that book, who knows what would've happened to the winter warmer."

8. Winter Solstice

Anderson Valley Brewing Company
Boonville, California
www.avbc.com
Style: Spiced **WINTER WARMER**
Alcohol volume: 6.9%
Serve with: Pumpkin pie

It all starts with the solstice, of course: the sun, at its lowest point, finally begins its climb back into the sky, the days lengthen, and the earth is reborn. Christmas beer can perhaps trace its roots to the ancient civilizations that celebrated the turning point in the yearly calendar, when masters and slaves in Rome reversed their roles in Saturnalia festivities, the Persians offered sacrifices to Mithra, and everyone drank alcohol to reach a happy, enlightened state. And it is no coincidence that many of the world's religions mark their biggest festivals at this time of the year. These days, however, in a world where you can buy fresh tomatoes in December and even our car seats are heated, the solstice goes by almost unnoticed. A sip of this creamy ale won't necessarily bring out your inner pagan, but it does provide a modest buzz and a warm sensation in your belly. The spices aren't overwhelming—perhaps some cinnamon—and it finishes with an understated cherry-vanilla flavor.

❆ • ❆ • ❆ • ❆ • ❆ • ❆ • ❆ • ❆ • ❆ • ❆ • ❆ • ❆ • ❆ • ❆ • ❆ • ❆ • ❆

Boonville's old-timers still speak a local dialect known as Boontling. If you hear someone describe a beer as "Bahl Hornin'," that means "good drinking."

9. Old Jubilation

Avery Brewing
Boulder, Colorado
www.averybrewing.com
Style: **ENGLISH STRONG ALE**
Alcohol volume: 8%
Serve with: Meatloaf

This brewery is known for its religious-themed beers, namely Salvation (a strong Belgian golden ale) and The Reverend (a quadruple), so you might be disappointed that it didn't come up with something similarly pious for the holidays. In fact, "jubilation" has its roots in the Bible, specifically Leviticus, where it states that the blowing of a ram's horn (*yobel* in Hebrew) marked the beginning of the Jubilee every fifty years. In that year, under religious law, debts were forgiven and slaves were freed. So while it's not exactly a Christmas theme, the spirit is the same. Old Jubilation is reddish brown and rich, and at first it seems to be a simple dark beer that's been flavored with toffee or perhaps pine. But there are no added spices, just a beautiful blend of five different specialty malts balanced nicely with English hops. The biggest surprise is how quickly it hits your head; with its light, easy-to-quaff body, you won't notice it contains 8 percent alcohol until you hear a ram's horn echoing in your ears.

Only very lucky beer drinkers can claim to have enjoyed Avery's first holiday beer. Brewed for just one year (1995), Raspberry Trufale was made with raspberries and chocolate.

10. Ringnes Julebokk

Ringnes Bryggeri
Oslo, Norway
www.ringnes.no
Style: **DOUBLE BOCK**
Alcohol volume: 9.9%
Serve with: Roasted duck

Americans who grouse about unusual state liquor laws should try buying a beer in Norway. Here's a nation of frozen fjords and twenty-four hours of darkness, a cold land where you'd presume that easy access to alcohol would be a necessity in the midst of winter. Instead, grocery stores are prohibited from selling anything more potent than 4.7 percent alcohol. This means that at Christmas the store shelves are lined with dumbed-down brownish suds, with little more character than the lame lagers sold during the rest of the year. For stronger stuff, you have to traipse off to the state-run liquor monopoly, Vinmonopolet (which, by the way, closes at 3 p.m. on Saturdays). But if you're lucky, you'll find one of the finest strong bocks in the world there. Ringnes Julebokk is somewhat sweet, with a clear, strong flavor of caramel followed by a spicy finish. And at nearly 10 percent alcohol, it will certainly keep you warm until the sun returns next spring.

❄·❄·❄·❄·❄·❄·❄·❄·❄·❄·❄·❄·❄·❄·❄·❄·❄·❄·❄·❄

During the holidays, Norwegians supplement their beer drinking with ample toasts of aquavit, a smooth but strong schnappslike digestif.

11. Delirium Noël

Brouwerij Huyghe
Melle, Belgium
www.delirium.be
Style: **BELGIAN STRONG DARK ALE**
Alcohol volume: 10%
Serve with: Duck salad

I hate to sound shallow, but this Belgian ale earns a place in this book for its label alone. There are actually several collectible versions of the artwork, all of them involving pink elephants in Santa hats, skiing or sledding on a white ceramic bottle. It's all very trippy, like one of those psychedelic dreams you get after a crumb of cheese. More to the point, the 750ml bottle makes an excellent gift, one that puts the recipient in a cheerful spirit even before uncorking. Inside you'll find a delicious dark brown ale, spiced with a sharp yeast bite and candy sugar. Pour it into a goblet, and you get a full-bodied quaff topped with a thick white head. Its maker, the one-hundred-year-old Huyghe brewery outside Ghent, is best known for what is easily the most non-politically correct brand ever packaged: Delirium Tremens.

❆ . ❆ . ❆ . ❆ . ❆ . ❆ . ❆ . ❆ . ❆ . ❆ . ❆ . ❆ . ❆ . ❆ . ❆ . ❆ . ❆ . ❆ . ❆ . ❆

Huyghe's Delirium Café in the Îlot Sacré section of Brussels is an excellent place to sample some Christmas beer. It stocks more than two thousand brands of all types.

12. Baladin Noël

Birrificio Le Baladin
Piozzo, Italy
www.birreria.com
Style: **BELGIAN STRONG DARK ALE**
Alcohol volume: 9%
Serve with: Hershey's Kisses

A great beer from Italy? That's a little like a fine wine from Canada, isn't it? This is the land of Chianti and Valpolicella, not stouts and porters, and when it turns to grain, the country typically produces innocuous industrial lagers like Moretti and Peroni. In fact, Italy might become the next great craft beer country, thanks largely to its burgeoning Slow Food movement, which emphasizes the use of local ingredients by artisans. Travel through Europe, and you'll surely meet Italian beer hunters looking for new styles to mimic and adapt for their own unique production. One of them, café owner Teo Musso, founded La Baladin brewpub after spending years learning everything he could about beer from the Belgians. Today he's one of the organizers of Union Birra, a consortium of northern Italian brewpubs. This ale is dark and deep, like a Barolo, with a vast array of dried fruit, cocoa, plum, and pepper flavors—much of it a product of yeast fermentation.

In Italy, children receive their holiday gifts on the night of January 5, the eve of Epiphany. On that night, a mythical woman named La Befana fills their stockings with candy and may even sweep the floor before she leaves.

13. Gouden Carolus Noël

Brouwerij Het Anker
Mechelen, Belgium
www.hetanker.be
Style: **BELGIAN STRONG DARK ALE**
Alcohol volume: 10.5%
Serve with: Pecan pie

When Charles V—aka Gouden Carolus—was ruler of the Holy Roman Empire in the mid-1500s, the Het Anker brewery that makes this ale in his hometown was already nearly two hundred years old. It's well known that the emperor preferred beer to wine. According to one legend, during a visit to the nearby village of Olen, he stopped by an inn for a cold drink. The innkeeper offered him a mug, holding it by the handle. The king refused to touch the stein and demanded a mug with two handles. The innkeeper returned, grasping the mug by both handles (even kings, apparently, have a tough time finding good help). Frustrated, the ruler handed the server a gold coin and told him to craft a mug with a third handle. Today you can find versions of the three-handled mug throughout Flanders—possibly the ideal glass for this kingly holiday ale. It's dark red and spiced with herbs, with a soft, creamy body that warms you from crown to toe.

☃ • ☃ • ☃ • ☃ • ☃ • ☃ • ☃ • ☃ • ☃ • ☃ • ☃ • ☃ • ☃ • ☃ • ☃ • ☃ • ☃ • ☃

When you're king of the world, you've got to watch your diet. Tests on the preserved pinkie of Charles V showed telltale signs of gout, the rich man's disease that is sometimes linked to excessive beer consumption.

14. La Binchoise Reserve Speciale

Brasserie La Binchoise

Binche, Belgium

www.brasserielabinchoise.be

Style: **BELGIAN STRONG PALE ALE**

Alcohol volume: 9%

Serve with: Port-Salut cheese

Imagine painting a masterpiece of the Virgin Mary and her child standing on a bank of clouds, being glorified by the saints. It is the essence of the Christmas story, a work of art that will endure for centuries— the Sistine Madonna. But then some dopey greeting card designer clips out a pair of dreamy-eyed angels from the bottom of the canvas, and suddenly they are more recognized than the painting itself. They begin to show up on posters, boxes of candy, key rings, neckties, wallpaper, postage stamps—and even this beer. They become so famous, the painting is renamed "Two Angels," and everyone forgets about Mary, Jesus, and the saints. If Raphael were still alive, we'd recommend this recourse: uncork this beer (called Cuvée Spécial Noël in Europe) and enjoy its spectacularly complex range of flavors, from sweet fruits to delicately bitter hops.

The two masked characters beneath the Binchoise flag on the label are "Gilles," *characters from the Carnival of Binche who have paraded through town annually on* *Shrove Tuesday since the fourteenth century.*

15. Corsendonk Christmas Ale

Brouwerij Corsendonk
Oud-Turnhout, Belgium
corsendonk.apluz.be
Style: **BELGIAN STRONG DARK ALE**
Alcohol volume: 8.5%
Serve with: Pasta primavera

Austrian Emperor Joseph II might have been the original scrooge. Among other decrees during his rule in the late eighteenth century, he banned the Viennese tradition of displaying crèches during the Christmas season. Never mind that the city held what is believed to be a fragment of Christ's manger—Joseph II was not a big fan of Catholic tradition. Indeed, in his anti-Vatican zeal, he started shutting down monasteries across Europe, including the famed Corsendonk priory in the lowlands outside Antwerp. Goodbye monks, goodbye beer: a brewery that had been producing fine ales for four centuries was confiscated. Thankfully, today the Corsendonk monastery has been restored and is open to guests. The beer that takes its name, however, is made approximately one hundred miles south, by Brasserie du Bocq, a well-regarded contract brewer. Its Christmas Ale might be the prototypical Belgian holiday brew: rich and dark with a spicy, chocolatey aroma and a smooth, flavorful body that has a fruitlike finish. Look for corked 25-ounce bottles nicely packaged in festive tin canisters.

❅ • ❅ • ❅ • ❅ • ❅ • ❅ • ❅ • ❅ • ❅ • ❅ • ❅ • ❅ • ❅ • ❅ • ❅ • ❅ • ❅ • ❅

The library at the Corsendonk priory was visited frequently by Erasmus, the Dutch theologian whose critical 1516 publication of the Greek New Testament helped popularize and humanize the works of Christ.

16. Mahr's Christmas Bock

Brauerei Mahr
Bamberg, Germany
www.mahrs-braeu.de
Style: **BOCK**
Alcohol volume: 6%
Serve with: Apple sausage

In Bavaria, when the Oktoberfest tents are folded up and the temperatures begin to dip, brewers prepare for the cold months ahead with rich, malty, dark batches of *stark*, or strong, beer. It's the first beer of the new brewing season, made with freshly harvested malt and hops. Traditionally, it's tapped just in time for the first day of Advent, in late November or early December. They've been doing this for centuries in Bamberg, a medieval town where the oldest breweries can trace their history to the early 1500s. Mahr's Brau is family owned and, by many accounts, the finest in town. The timber-beamed dining room of Mahr's *gastrube* is a comfortable place to enjoy this delicately balanced bock, but you're more likely to find locals hanging out in the brewery's standing-only section, or *schwemme*. The first time this festive beer was offered, the crowd—known as *stehgammler* (loafers)—sucked down the entire supply in two hours.

※ • ※ • ※ • ※ • ※ • ※ • ※ • ※ • ※ • ※ • ※ • ※ • ※ • ※ • ※ • ※ • ※ • ※

Bamberg, protected by UNESCO as a World Heritage Site, is the scene of an annual Trail of Nativity Scenes during the Christmas season. Visitors can barhop while following a walking tour of thirty-four nativities around town.

17. Affligem Noël

Brouwerij Affligem
Opwijk, Belgium
www.affligembeer.be
Style: **BELGIAN DUBBEL**
Alcohol volume: 9%
Serve with: Roast turkey and stuffing

I went into a deep funk a few years ago when this beer was temporarily pulled from the U.S. market in a dispute over distribution rights. The dispute not only interrupted a heritage that goes back almost one thousand years, it also forced me to break into an emergency case I'd been hiding in the basement, behind my dusty old Lionel train set. The good news is that it ages wonderfully: dark brown and savory, like bread in a bottle. The better news is that it's back on the shelves. Pour a glass and dive into the foamy white head, and you'll get big, sweet chocolate and caramel flavors—a product of the malt that is grown on the Affligem abbey's own fields. But let it warm in the goblet and discover thick, complex layers of honey, buttered toast, nutmeg, plums, sugar fairies— I'm dreaming!

❦ · ❦ · ❦ · ❦ · ❦ · ❦ · ❦ · ❦ · ❦ · ❦ · ❦ · ❦ · ❦ · ❦ · ❦ · ❦ · ❦ · ❦

The Affligem abbey was founded in 1074 by six knights who gave up their life of pillaging, sacking, and carousing to adopt the peaceful monastic principles (and brewing) of the Benedictines.

18. Hibernation Ale

Great Divide Brewing
Denver, Colorado
www.greatdivide.com
Style: **OLD ALE**
Alcohol volume: 8.1%
Serve with: Aged gouda

Why don't human beings hibernate? I don't mean just bundling up on the couch for a weekend of NFL playoff games. I'm talking lower body temperature, reduced heart rate, Yogi Bear–like sonic snoring—total shutdown. It would be great to just sleep through the cold months and wake up refreshed in time for bock season. In fact, scientists are busy at work on artificial hibernation inducement (presumably so we can travel to Mars, and not so we can avoid shoveling the sidewalk). In the meantime I suggest a sixpack of this metabolism-altering ale. Brewed in July while it's still toasty outside, Hibernation is made with five different malts and three varieties of hops. Then it's aged for three months to mellow out a complex variety of flavors: brown sugar, toffee, dried fruit, and roasted malt. No, it won't send you into total hibernation, but it should at least get you through the holidays with the in-laws.

❆ · ❆ · ❆ · ❆ · ❆ · ❆ · ❆ · ❆ · ❆ · ❆ · ❆ · ❆ · ❆ · ❆ · ❆ · ❆ · ❆ · ❆

Fans of massive Christmas light displays head to the Denver Botanic Gardens, where more than one million twinkling lights decorate plants and trees across its seventeen acres.

19. Santa's Private Reserve Ale

Rogue Ales Brewery
Newport, Oregon
www.rogue.com
Style: **RED ALE**
Alcohol volume: 6%
Serve with: New England clam chowder

In Clement Clarke Moore's famous poem in 1823, the right jolly old elf St. Nicholas raised a finger to his nose before ascending the chimney. In many cultures, it's the sign of a secret—perhaps accompanied by a wink. But Santa with a raised, clenched fist? Head brewer John Maier has made this defiant fist a symbol of Rogue's rebellious ales. And perhaps the raised fist on this bottle is appropriate nonetheless: there are no secret ingredients in this ale, just a full sack of hops, including Chinook, Centennial, and a variety that Maier calls "Rudolph." Its deep red color hints at a bit of sweetness in the malt. You'll be tempted to drink more than one in a sitting—if you can peel it from Santa's clutch.

❄ • ❄ • ❄ • ❄ • ❄ • ❄ • ❄ • ❄ • ❄ • ❄ • ❄ • ❄ • ❄ • ❄ • ❄ • ❄ • ❄ • ❄ • ❄ • ❄

The 22-ounce bottle is decorated with glistening, glow-in-the-dark snowflakes.

20. Smuttynose Winter Ale

Smuttynose Brewing
Portsmouth, New Hampshire
www.smuttynose.com
Style: **BELGIAN DUBBEL**
Alcohol volume: 6.8%
Serve with: Cheeseburgers

Who is that mysterious woman on the label supposed to be? Mom coming home through a snowstorm with dinner? A neighbor carrying a box of cookies? Not even the folks at Smuttynose know. The photo is copyright-free clipart that the brewery plucked from a photography archive for the label. If you recognize her, contact Smuttynose—they might give you a free beer! Beneath that label is another little mystery: a handsome, full-flavored ale. It's a sweet, dark beer, much like a Belgian dubbel, but it's nowhere near that strong. Brewer David Yarrington was looking for the complex flavor of a strong ale, but without all that alcohol—something without spices that you could drink all night. He succeeds nicely with a Belgian ale yeast that produces a thoroughly enjoyable flavor of cherries, chocolate, and malt.

❆ • ❆ • ❆ • ❆ • ❆ • ❆ • ❆ • ❆ • ❆ • ❆ • ❆ • ❆ • ❆ • ❆ • ❆ • ❆ • ❆ • ❆

Smuttynose takes its name from one of a group of islands off the coast of New Hampshire that is most famous for a pair of grisly nineteenth-century ax murders.

21. Alpha Klaus

Three Floyds Brewing
Munster, Indiana
www.threefloyds.com
Style: **PORTER**
Alcohol volume: 7.5%
Serve with: Flank steak and grilled onions

That's one freaky tattooed Santa on this label—a sure sign of an offbeat beer. Three Floyds may be the ultimate cult brewery in America, nestled in northwest Indiana in the suburban sprawl around Lake Michigan. Its limited-production brands are distributed in only a handful of midwestern and eastern states. Its flagship, Alpha King, will challenge the palates of all but the most devoted of hopheads. Still, the brewery is so beloved that any time a new shipment shows up at a distributor, word spreads quickly and the bottles disappear in hours. The Floyds—Nick, his brother Simon, and their father Mike—amped up that brew, darkening it with chocolate malt and tossing in even more "strange American hops." The result is a wholly American-style porter that is festive in the same vein as Dan Aykroyd in his crusty Santa outfit in *Trading Places*. A 22-ounce bomber lives up to the brewery's reputation for producing "not normal" beers.

❆ • ❆ • ❆ • ❆ • ❆ • ❆ • ❆ • ❆ • ❆ • ❆ • ❆ • ❆ • ❆ • ❆ • ❆ • ❆ • ❆

It's just a five-hour drive south from the brewery to Santa Claus, Indiana.
Yes, that's a real town, and it is home to Santa's Candy Castle.

22. Winter-Traum

Klosterbrauerei Weltenburg

Kelheim, Germany

www.weltenburger.de

Style: **MARZEN**

Alcohol volume: 5.4%

Serve with: Hummus and pita bread

Other beers in this book may claim a connection to age-old monasteries, but this excellent, light-bodied lager is actually made by monks. And not just any order. The seventeen Benedictine brothers of the Weltenburg monastery trace their roots back to AD 600, when it was founded by Irish monks along the banks of the Danube. The brewery is relatively modern: a mere 950 years old (with production interrupted only by that notorious French wine snob, Napoleon). It has been rebuilt over the years with modern equipment, but they're still using the three-hundred-year-old lagering rooms nearly ten stories underground. Enter the monastery today and you're greeted with symbolic representations of the Four Last Things: Death, Judgment, Heaven, and Hell. Walk a little further, and you're greeted by the four ingredients of beer: water, malt, hops, and yeast. Together in Winter-Traum (Winter Dream), they combine to produce an astonishingly complex aroma of fresh citrus and spice, and a delicious flavor of freshly baked bread. Drink up before you encounter the other four.

❆ • ❆ • ❆ • ❆ • ❆ • ❆ • ❆ • ❆ • ❆ • ❆ • ❆ • ❆ • ❆ • ❆ • ❆ • ❆ • ❆ • ❆ • ❆

How do we know the brewery is so old? An ancient text, the Weltenburg Nekrologium, *documents the date of the original brewmaster's demise.*

23. Scaldis Noël

Brasserie Dubuisson Frères
Pipaix, Belgium
www.bush-beer.com
Style: **BELGIAN STRONG DARK ALE**
Alcohol volume: 12%
Serve with: Belgian truffles

"We're not about to make a light beer," a representative from Dubuisson Frères once told me. "It's just not in our DNA." And so this family-owned Wallonian brewer proudly proclaims its ultra-strong beer is "deliciously strooth" and "reassuringly smong." And that's after just one bottle. A generous batch of caramel malt gives this beer a pleasant copper-red color, and the sugar kicks it into high gear. You'd expect it to be overly sweet and cloying, but the hops balance it nicely, thanks partly to an extra dose of Saaz flowers added in the final stages of fermentation. The bottom line is that Scaldis Noël is dangerously drinkable. With its Champagne-like texture, the temptation is to gulp. Instead, pour it into a brandy snifter and sip it slowly while contemplating the embers in the fireplace. Look for it in unfiltered 750ml bottles, which are a bit fruitier (and perhaps a bit higher in alcohol).

❆ • ❆ • ❆ • ❆ • ❆ • ❆ • ❆ • ❆ • ❆ • ❆ • ❆ • ❆ • ❆ • ❆ • ❆ • ❆ • ❆ • ❆

This beer's original name is Bush de Noël, but under pressure from a certain St. Louis brewery whose first name is Anheuser, Dubuisson changed the name for the U.S. market to Scaldis, the Latin name for Belgium's famous Schelde River.

24. Winter White Ale

Bell's Brewery
Comstock, Michigan
www.bellsbeer.com
Style: **BELGIAN WITBIER**
Alcohol volume: 5%
Serve with: Steamed mussels

You'll notice a preponderance of so-called Big Beers in this book: heavy, dark, high-alcohol, richly flavored, malty monsters. I mean, why not? It's winter, time to bulk up. And you'd be forgiven if you expected the same kind of gigantism from the likes of Larry Bell's highly regarded brewery. After all, he bottles no fewer than five different stouts that are perfectly warming on a cold winter's night. So what does Bell's offer as a way of holiday celebration? A spritzer! Well, not exactly; this witbier—or white beer—is light and effervescent. But beneath that cloudy texture is the aroma of coriander and citrus. It's made with a house blend of German hefeweizen and Belgian yeasts, which combine to produce a curious layering of flavors. No, you might not down this in a blizzard. Think of it as an aperitif before you settle into those other Big Beers.

❆ · ❆ · ❆ · ❆ · ❆ · ❆ · ❆ · ❆ · ❆ · ❆ · ❆ · ❆ · ❆ · ❆ · ❆ · ❆ · ❆ · ❆

Bell's began life as a homebrewing supply shop.

25. 2° Below Ale

New Belgium Brewing
Fort Collins, Colorado
www.newbelgium.com
Style: **EXTRA SPECIAL BITTER**
Alcohol volume: 6.6%
Serve with: Lamb kebabs

New Belgium keeps the Christmas spirit year-round: it's environmentally responsible, it shares profits with its employees, and it raises money for the needy. Though Fat Tire, a basic amber ale, is its best-known beer, the brewery also produces a highly regarded series of specialty ales that challenge the taste buds. Oddly, though, when New Belgium first launched 2° Below, many of its biggest fans reacted with a big thumbs-down. "Too weird" was the classic comment. I disagree. This is an exceptional ale that shouldn't be missed. Its pinkish-copper body is capped by a nice, snowy mound of foam. There's a brilliant clarity in the glass—the result, says the brewery, of chilling the beer in its final stage to -2°C. The hop aroma reminds me of a freshly cut Christmas tree, thanks to dry hopping with Sterling and Liberty hops. On your first swallow, though, you get a creamy mouthful of toasty malt goodness with a slight, tingly bite of chocolate. And just below the surface, what is that flavor? Why, it tastes like Fat Tire would if it had been touched by angels.

New Belgium also makes Frambozen, another specialty ale that's available only during the holidays. It's a brown ale made with real raspberries—perfect with a cheese course or dessert.

26. La Dragonne

BFM Brasserie des Franches-Montagnes
Saignelégier, Switzerland
www.brasseriebfm.ch
Style: **SPICED WINTER WARMER ALE**
Alcohol volume: 4%
Serve with: Pfeffernüsse cookies

Throughout Germany in December, Christmas markets sparkle with decorations, gingerbread cookies called Lebkuchen, and cups of steaming, spiced glühwein. Brewer Jérôme Rebetez, who started out as a winemaker, took his cues from that warming beverage and came up with this: a hot mulled ale. And I don't mean warm, like those British ales that American tourists complain about. I mean: dunk the bottle into a boiling pot of water and leave it there for about five minutes until the contents reach 130°F; then grab a potholder, crack open the bottle, and pour it into a sturdy glass. The sensation and the flavor are unlike those of any other beer: honey, cinnamon, anise, orange peel, cloves, cardamom, coriander, juniper—basically the entire contents of your spice cabinet. Take a deep sip and the aroma rushes through your head. This is a beer to enjoy after an afternoon on the ski slopes. Or even in a thermos on the lift.

❅ · ❅ · ❅ · ❅ · ❅ · ❅ · ❅ · ❅ · ❅ · ❅ · ❅ · ❅ · ❅ · ❅ · ❅ · ❅ · ❅ · ❅ · ❅

Located in the Jura Mountains along the northwestern border of Switzerland,
Brasserie Des Franches-Montagnes hand-bottles all of its beers.

27. Ebenezer Ale

BridgePort Brewing
Portland, Oregon
www.bridgeportbrew.com
Style: **WINTER WARMER**
Alcohol volume: 6.4%
Serve with: Grispelles (Italian fish donuts)

Sixpacks of this smooth-drinking ale are decorated with the two sides of Dickens's archetypal character: the mean-spirited Scrooge on one, and the philanthropic Ebenezer on the other. Scrooge, of course, has become a synonym for miserliness. And Ebenezer? The name is found in the Bible as a Hebrew word referring to the stone that marked the site where the Israelites took back the Ark of the Covenant. Ebenezer means "stone of help," but more literally it's a reminder of God's presence. Some believe Dickens intended a hidden meaning in Scrooge's surname, but the author cribbed the name from a grave marker for a grain merchant that he saw in Scotland: "Here lies Ebenezer Lennox Scroggie—meal man." Dickens misread it as "mean man," and, well, you can read the rest of the story over a pint of this malty copper-hued brew.

* * *

> *"I am as giddy as a drunken man!"*
> —*Ebenezer Scrooge in* A Christmas Carol

28. La Choulette de Noël

Brasserie la Choulette
Hordain, France
www.lachoulette.com
Style: **BIERE DE GARDE**
Alcohol volume: 7%
Serve with: Light salad

In northern France near the border of Belgium, where grapes don't grow that easily, farmers use the region's barley to craft a drink called *bière de garde*. That's "beer to keep," because it's made in early spring and laid down through the hot summer months when it's too hot to brew. Though it was originally brewed to help cool off the farmhands, it's very much like a good wine whose flavor is enhanced when served with a wide range of foods, from stinky cheese to roasted goose. The style shares much with Belgium's saison, including a distinctive yeast that produces fruity and herbal notes. In this version, you'll notice the yeast sediment in the bottle; either carefully decant the bottle, or mix it into your glass (go ahead, it won't bite you). The flavor is sweet, with a satisfying medium body of malt nuttiness. La Choulette is a rustic brewery, dating back to 1845. All of its styles are meticulously brewed and stand as proof that the French know how to make more than just wine.

❅ • ❅ • ❅ • ❅ • ❅ • ❅ • ❅ • ❅ • ❅ • ❅ • ❅ • ❅ • ❅ • ❅ • ❅

Choulette *is the wooden ball used in a traditional regional game called* crosse.

29. St. Nikolaus Bock Bier

Pennsylvania Brewing Company
Pittsburgh, Pennsylvania
www.pennbrew.com
Style: **BOCK**
Alcohol volume: 7.5%
Serve with: Venison

Made with five different roasted malts, this smooth-tasting, chocolatey, dark Munich-style lager is one of the world's classic bocks. Like the other fine beers in this book, it's available only in the wintertime. But to get a true taste of St. Nicholas, you have to go to the Italian town of Bari, where they bottle the holy Manna of St. Nikolaus in the spring. On May 9, the Feast of the Translation, the rector extracts a mysterious transparent liquid that seeps from the crypt holding the saint's bones. No one is certain what produces the liquid, but devotees say it has the power to heal. Only an ounce or so is extracted and bottled in a hand-painted flask. It's then diluted in holy water and distributed to believers, who either rub it on their bodies or drink it down. Yes, that's right, they drink the bodily essence of St. Nick. If you're looking for something a bit more palatable, try the Brewer's Reserve version of this bock. The 25-ounce bottle is a bit stronger at 9 percent alcohol and is packed in an embroidered velvet bag.

The character on the label is "Merry Old Santa Claus," by Thomas Nast, which appeared in Harper's Weekly *in 1881—one of the earliest illustrations of Santa in America.*

30. St. Feuillien Cuvée de Noël

Brasserie St. Feuillien
Le Roeulx, Belgium
www.st-feuillien.com
Style: **BELGIAN STRONG DARK ALE**
Alcohol volume: 9%
Serve with: Crab hors d'oeuvres

There's nothing like showing up at a holiday party with a Salmanazar—that's the name for those 9-liter bottles about the size of an ICBM nosecone. Believe me, you attract a lot of attention when you've got that much beer in your arms. Aside from the pure fun of attempting to glug-glug-glug the contents into a tiny 8-ounce goblet, there actually is a benefit to packaging beer in such a large bottle: all that liquid decreases the proportionate amount of oxygen. And oxygen is bad for beer. It gives it a stale flavor and, for a dark ale like Cuvée de Noël, turns the rich malt aroma into something more like sweetened sherry. Though you're more likely to encounter St. Feuillien's beautiful plumlike Christmas beer in much smaller 33cl bottles, it pays to track down the big boys. Look for a magnum (1.5 liters), jeroboam (3 liters), Methuselah (6 liters), or the fabled Salmanazar, which equals more than an entire case of beer in a single bottle.

᳄ · ᳄ · ᳄ · ᳄ · ᳄ · ᳄ · ᳄ · ᳄ · ᳄ · ᳄ · ᳄ · ᳄ · ᳄ · ᳄ · ᳄ · ᳄ · ᳄ · ᳄ · ᳄

St. Feuillien takes its name from a martyred Irish monk who was slain by outlaws, decapitated, and buried in a pig sty in Le Roeulx.

31. Jenlain Noël

Brasserie Duyck
Jenlain, France
www.duyck.com
Style: **BIERE DE GARDE**
Alcohol volume: 6.8%
Serve with: Chevre or Tomme de Savoie cheese

Until the 1900s, Nord-Pas-de-Calais, the region around this brewery, drank beer, not wine. Some two thousand breweries produced fresh, cloudy ales that were not unlike the saison and farmhouse ales made just to the north, in Belgium. Then the Kaiser's armies rolled through during World War I and removed most of the equipment. Twenty years later, Hitler's forces did the same. Today they drink Bordeaux in Lille and turn up their noses at German beer. Brasserie Duyck, one of the area's few breweries to survive the wars, celebrates the season with its Noël, a ramped-up version of its superb flagship Ambrée. It contains more malt and more hops, but, in the tradition of many European brewers, no added price. The nonpasteurized beer is a fun, billowing foamster with lots of flowery aroma and a touch of spice and fruit.

Duyck is one of the original recyclers. After World War II, it began selling its beer in used Champagne bottles brought to the brewery by its customers.

32. Hitachino Nest Commemorative Ale

Kiuchi Brewery

Kounosu, Japan

www.kodawari.cc

Style: **SPICED ICE BOCK**

Alcohol volume: 9%

Serve with: Japanese Christmas sponge cake
(with strawberries and whipped cream)

In Japan, where Shinto and Buddhism are the predominant religions, Christmas is not a huge national holiday. Instead, New Year's Day is the big event. People send postcards to friends, decorate their houses, give pocket money and small gifts to children, prepare festive meals, and, of course, drink beer. Most of the big breweries produce a winter beer called *fuyumonogatari* ("winter tale") in cans decorated with winter scenes. It's only mildly stronger than the run-of-the-mill pale lagers that dominate the marketplace, so for something special you have to track down a beer from one of Japan's new wave of microbreweries. This one is an ice bock, a style that gets its name from an old process in which, after fermentation, the beer is chilled to 24°F, allowing the water (but not the alcohol) to freeze. The ice is then removed, which both sharpens the flavor and increases the alcohol content. Spiced with coriander, nutmeg, ginger, and cinnamon, this is a truly imaginative and unique beer.

33. Doggie Claws

Hair of the Dog Brewing Company
Portland, Oregon
www.hairofthedog.com
Style: **BARLEYWINE**
Alcohol volume: 11.5%
Serve with: Stilton cheese

The morning after you made a fool of yourself at the office holiday party, you might be tempted to cure that hangover with a little hair of the dog that bit you. The idea, of course, is that a little more of what caused your headache might actually ease it. The phrase is derived from a literal cure—at one time, people tried to cure rabies by spreading dog hair on the wound. It goes back to Hippocrates, the great physician, and the philosophy of *similia similibus curantur* ("like cures like"). Does it work? Well, a good jolt in the morning might take off the edge, but only momentarily; all you've done is add even more toxins that your body has to break down. So take a moment to reflect before grabbing a bottle of Doggie Claws in the morning. In fact, watch out the night before. This is a barleywine: a hoppy beer brewed to the strength of wine. If you gulp this sweet, thick, and creamy ale too quickly, it'll bite back.

❆ • ❆ • ❆ • ❆ • ❆ • ❆ • ❆ • ❆ • ❆ • ❆ • ❆ • ❆ • ❆ • ❆ • ❆ • ❆ • ❆ • ❆ • ❆

If you show up at the brewery on the day it releases Doggie Claws, make sure you also grab one of the very rare cases of Fred from the Wood. It's a hoppy ale, aged six months in oak barrels, and named after Portland beer writer Fred Eckhardt.

34. St. Bernardus Christmas Ale

Brouwerij St. Bernardus
Watou, Belgium
www.sintbernardus.be
Style: **BELGIAN STRONG DARK ALE**
Alcohol volume: 10%
Serve with: Chimay cheese

There's a happy monk on the label—probably a rendition of St. Bernard of Clairvaux, the twelfth-century cleric who revived the Benedictine monastery movement. Such a strong, fortifying beer, though, ought to recall an even more famous St. Bernard—the one who lent his name to the barrel-toting St. Bernard dog. Though he isn't exactly a church hero, St. Bernard of Menthon is famous for establishing a monastery in the mid-tenth century along a treacherous Alpine pass that was frequently traversed by pilgrims on their way to Rome. The locals trained the big dogs to bound through the snow, pluck out those who'd gotten trapped, and as the myth goes provide them with a taste of brandy. At 10 percent alcohol, this dark, chocolatey ale would do the trick, too. It's marvelously spicy, with a deep flavor of raisins. And what about St. Bernard of Clairvaux? He's known notoriously for helping to launch the bloody Second Crusade in 1145—on Christmas Day.

St. Bernardus is owned by a family named Claus.

35. Heavy Seas Winter Storm

Clipper City Brewery
Baltimore, Maryland
www.ccbeer.com
Style: **EXTRA SPECIAL BITTER**
Alcohol volume: 7.5%
Serve with: Cheese ravioli

The five categories of winter storms are Notable, Significant, Major, Crippling, and Extreme. Calling itself a "Category 5," this winter beer from Clipper City Brewing is, in fact, extreme. And I mean that as praise, in the same way a ten-year-old kid thinks twenty inches of snow on a school day is a good thing. It's supposed to be an extra special bitter, where the malt balances the bitterness to produce an easy-sipping all-nighter. But this ale features no fewer than five different hop varieties, including those northwestern darlings, Cascade, Centennial, and Chinook. You'll find an underlying sweet malt base that tones down the tang a bit, but with all these aromatic hops, that's a little like saying the sun was shining until that massive nor'easter barreled down the coast and shut down I-95.

When the storm breaks, grab a sixpack and head over to the fantastic lighting display on 34th Street, known as Christmas Street, in the Hampden section of Baltimore. You can get your picture taken with a beer-swilling "New Year's Baby."

36. Goose Island Christmas Ale

Goose Island Beer

Chicago, Illinois

www.gooseisland.com

Style: **BROWN ALE**

Alcohol volume: 5.6%

Serve with: Pork with spiced apples

Three days before Christmas in 1887, three dozen Chicago breweries took out an advertisement in *The Tribune* to announce some bad news: "In view of the present low price of beer, as well as the high-priced material and labor, the undersigned have resolved to abandon the habit of making Christmas presents." Traditionally, taverns could expect to receive as many as ten half-barrels of suds for the holidays. One newsman found "proprietors greatly heated around the collar" over the manifesto. "I work the flesh off my bones for these robbers and now they knock me out of the Christmas *geschenk* [gift]," griped one. Well, payback is a bitch: in the next century, every one of those scrooge-like brewers would go belly-up. And today? You won't find any free beer in Chicago, but you can get a wonderful taste of the holidays from the Second City's Goose Island. The brewery tweaks the recipe of its Christmas Ale each year, but typically it features a nutlike aroma, with a chewy, full-bodied, breadlike flavor.

❧ . ❧ . ❧ . ❧ . ❧ . ❧ . ❧ . ❧ . ❧ . ❧ . ❧ . ❧ . ❧ . ❧ . ❧ . ❧ . ❧ . ❧

The Walnut Room at Macy's in downtown Chicago is one of the best places to get into the holiday spirit (or take a breather while the kids visit Santa). Grab a drink and enjoy the decorations beneath the department store's enormous Christmas tree.

37. Petrus Winterbeer

Brouwerij Bavik
Bavikhove, Belgium
www.bavik.be
Style: **BELGIAN STRONG DARK ALE**
Alcohol volume: 7%
Serve with: Prime rib

The jolly old gent on this label has always reminded me of one of America's great holiday-season advertising icons: the Norelco Santa. You remember him—the animated character who rode across the snowy landscape atop an electric razor. Strange—why would a guy with a snow-white beard endorse a razor, anyway? It's something to contemplate after cracking open a bottle of this fine, full-bodied ale. Under its thick, creamy head of foam, you'll find a smooth, clean-tasting brew that's a bit lighter than your standard Belgian Christmas treat. Still, it offers up that distinctive malt sweetness and warming afterglow. Petrus takes its name from the Latin name for St. Peter, the disciple of Jesus who, according to Catholic tradition, founded the first Christian church in Rome. I don't think he had any use for a Norelco razor, either.

※ • ※ • ※ • ※ • ※ • ※ • ※ • ※ • ※ • ※ • ※ • ※ • ※ • ※ • ※ • ※ • ※

Bavik is best known for the huge wooden vessels that it uses to condition its Old Brown ale. Some suspect that Winterbeer contains a touch of that tart aged beer.

38. Longfellow Winter Ale

Shipyard Brewing

Portland, Maine

www.shipyard.com

Style: **PORTER**

Alcohol volume: 5.8%

Serve with: Gorgonzola cheese

On Christmas Day 1864, Henry Wadsworth Longfellow greeted the holiday full of despair and grief: his beloved wife had died in a fire, his nation was at war, and his son was recovering from a battle wound. America's greatest poet sat down and wrote seven bittersweet stanzas that would become the lyrics to the season's most tearful carol, "I Heard the Bells on Christmas Day." The words are mainly forgotten today, as the carol plays endlessly on Muzak. In the poem Longfellow damns the world, crying, "There is no peace on earth . . . for hate is strong." But as he hears the bells peal, they remind all that "God is not dead, nor doth He sleep. The wrong shall fail, the right prevail." It's a hopeful sentiment worth reflecting upon when you have a moment to yourself. Grab a bottle of Shipyard's fine porter, find a quiet place in the midst of all the holiday mania, and read your Longfellow.

❆ • ❆ • ❆ • ❆ • ❆ • ❆ • ❆ • ❆ • ❆ • ❆ • ❆ • ❆ • ❆ • ❆ • ❆ • ❆ • ❆ • ❆ • ❆

Shipyard's brewery is built on the site of Longfellow's birthplace.

39. Kerst Pater

Brouwerij Van den Bossche
Sint-Lievens-Esse, Belgium
www.brouwerijvandenbossche.be
Style: **BELGIAN STRONG DARK ALE**
Alcohol volume: 9%
Serve with: Cougnou (sweet bread formed
 like a baby Jesus)

This brand name is Dutch for "Father Christmas," a nice, festive image. Except the "father" figure on this label from the Van den Bossche brewery actually refers to the patron saint of the local parish: Pater Lieven, or St. Livinus. Anyone familiar with the works of painter Peter Paul Rubens knows that the story of this saint is hardly one of good holiday cheer. Livinus, a monk who was bishop of Ghent, was martyred when Protestants sliced his tongue from his mouth; legend has it that the tongue continued preaching on its own. Rubens's masterpiece painting of the martyrdom, however, shows one of the assailants feeding the tongue to a dog—a gruesome image that nonetheless will not prevent me from making a bad joke about this ale's, uh, palate. Light-bodied with notes of fruit, chocolate, and coffee—you can't lick it.

※·※·※·※·※·※·※·※·※·※·※·※·※·※·※·※·※·※·※·※

In Belgium, St. Nicholas makes his first visit during the holiday season on December 4. That's the day he checks to see who's naughty or nice.

40. Samuel Adams Old Fezziwig

Boston Beer
Boston, Massachusetts
www.samueladams.com
Style: **SPICED WINTER WARMER**
Alcohol volume: 5.9%
Serve with: Gingerbread cookies

"Why, it's old Fezziwig! Bless his heart; it's Fezziwig alive again." Of all the scenes in Dickens's classic *A Christmas Carol*, the one in which Scrooge, with the ghost of Christmas Past, encounters his old boss is surely the most delightful—and heartbreaking. Fezziwig is the antithesis of Scrooge, a joyous, generous businessman loved by his employees. And he knew how to throw a party: "There was cake, and there was negus, and there was a great piece of Cold Roast, and was a great piece of Cold Boiled, and there were mince-pies, and plenty of beer." Unable to join in, the misbegotten Scrooge looks on, aware of how much he has lost. This ale would have fit in perfectly at Fezziwig's office party. Like negus (wine flavored with lemon, sugar, and spices), it is spiced with Saigon cinnamon and fresh ginger. The flavor is more like a well-balanced English bitter, with a honeylike malt flavor and a bit of orange in the finish.

❆ • ❆ • ❆ • ❆ • ❆ • ❆ • ❆ • ❆ • ❆ • ❆ • ❆ • ❆ • ❆ • ❆ • ❆ • ❆ • ❆ • ❆

Samuel Adams produces two other cold-weather brands: Winter Lager, a wheat bock spiced with ginger, cinnamon, and orange; and Cranberry Lambic, made with cranberries and spices.

41. Alaskan Winter Ale

Alaskan Brewing
Juneau, Alaska
www.alaskanbeer.com
Style: **WINTER WARMER**
Alcohol volume: 6.4%
Serve with: Cranberry nut bread

Only in the last five hundred years or so has hops been the favored ingredient to bitter and balance beer. Until the 1500s, brewers used all kinds of plant life—mushrooms, tree bark, seeds, flowers, you name it—with varying degrees of success. Even after hops became widely used, beer makers—especially those in colder regions where the vine doesn't prosper—turned to other products from Mother Nature. Unable to purchase hops, early American brewers followed a recipe popularized by Benjamin Franklin for spruce-flavored beer, and that's the secret ingredient in this one, a classic English old ale flavored with Sitka spruce tips. Just dip your nose into a goblet and you're greeted with a delicate floral aroma. At first sip, it may be hard to distinguish their flavor from your favorite Northwest hops variety. Don't be tempted to try to homebrew a batch with your Christmas tree, though. Spruce tips are the succulent, lime-colored new growth on the ends of branches, and you won't find them amid all that tinsel.

❆·❆

Each winter, Alaskan also releases its renowned Smoked Porter made with malt that is smoked for three days over alder wood at a local salmon smokehouse.

42. Geary's Winter Ale

D.L. Geary Brewing
Portland, Maine
www.gearybrewing.com
Style: **INDIA PALE ALE**
Alcohol volume: 6%
Serve with: Cold shrimp with Old Bay seasoning

Geary's, the oldest microbrewery in New England, used to brew one of the three best Christmas beers made in America, Hampshire Special Ale—"Only available," the brewery famously proclaimed, "when the weather sucks!" A well-balanced, full-flavored strong English ale, it drew fans from all along the Atlantic Coast and accounted for a quarter of the brewery's annual sales—it was that good. Its popularity was impossible to ignore, so a few years ago Geary's began to brew it year-round, sucky weather or not. Which is nice, I suppose, but it's no longer so special. We're left with this new wintertime beer, a very good IPA. It pours bright orange with an aroma that is quite floral. I'm guessing that's the work of one of my favorite hops: Fuggles. (Not because of their flavor; I just love saying Fuggles.) This is a very enjoyable bottle, but had the brewery stuck with HSA for the holidays, you would've seen Geary's about thirty entries sooner in this list.

❈ · ❈ · ❈ · ❈ · ❈ · ❈ · ❈ · ❈ · ❈ · ❈ · ❈ · ❈ · ❈ · ❈ · ❈ · ❈ · ❈ · ❈

Portland, one of America's best beer cities, was also the birthplace of Prohibition.
In 1851, its mayor, Neal S. Dow, known as the "Napoleon of Temperance," led a successful
campaign to make Maine the first dry state in the nation.

43. Snow Goose Winter Ale

Wild Goose Brewery
Frederick, Maryland
www.wildgoosebrewery.com
Style: **STRONG ENGLISH ALE**
Alcohol volume: 6.2%
Serve with: Roasted goose

Somehow I suspect the folks who named this beer were unaware that its namesake is one of the biggest feathered pests in North America. Less than one hundred years ago, it was an endangered species, and hunters were arrested for shooting at the massive winged beast. Today, thanks largely to plentiful food and global warming, it's thriving. And now it's eating everything in sight, wiping out large swaths of wetlands and screwing up salinity levels along the coasts. Do your part: consume Snow Goose Winter Ale immediately. The aroma is all Fuggles, thanks to dry hopping. The flavor is roasted toffee, with a hint of spice. It's famously fermented with Ringwood yeast, giving it a dry finish that makes this an easy sipper.

❄ • ❄ • ❄ • ❄ • ❄ • ❄ • ❄ • ❄ • ❄ • ❄ • ❄ • ❄ • ❄ • ❄ • ❄ • ❄ • ❄ • ❄ • ❄

"Bob said he didn't believe there ever was such a goose cooked. Its tenderness and flavor, size, and cheapness, were the themes of universal admiration."
—*Charles Dickens,* A Christmas Carol

44. Père Noël

Brouwerij De Ranke

Wevelgem, Belgium

www.deranke.be

Style: **BELGIAN STRONG PALE ALE**

Alcohol volume: 7%

Serve with: Lobster bisque

Père Noël is "Father Christmas" in French, the language of Belgium's Wallonia region, but the French Santa looks nothing like this label's red-suited guy. Père Noël usually wears a long red robe with a hood. And that's not the only thing that's out of place. This bottle is made in Belgium's West Flanders, a region where you get coal in your stocking for speaking French instead of Flemish. And the beer? It's a dry, hoppy ale—not the usual sweet, malty brew you'd expect from Belgium. But why nitpick? This is still a complex beer meant to be savored. Hopheads might be disappointed because there's little of that full-frontal wallop. But let it warm a bit and take a long, full pull: there are subtle flavors of spice here that will surprise you if you give it a chance.

❧ • ❧ • ❧ • ❧ • ❧ • ❧ • ❧ • ❧ • ❧ • ❧ • ❧ • ❧ • ❧ • ❧ • ❧ • ❧ • ❧ • ❧ • ❧

When Père Noël makes his visits, he is accompanied by Le Père Fouettard,
the grimy character who hands out coal to naughty kids.

45. Old Man Winter Ale

Southern Tier Brewing
Lakewood, New York
www.southerntierbrewing.com
Style: **OLD ALE**
Alcohol volume: 8%
Serve with: Dessert cheese plate

In Russia, they call Old Man Winter "Morozko." As the story goes, a wicked woman sends her stepdaughter into the cold to freeze to death. But when she meets Morozko, instead of shivering, she greets him warmly. Pleased by her spirit, the wintry specter gives her a blanket to stay warm, along with jewels and gifts, which she brings back to her home. The woman, hoping to strike it rich, sends her own daughter into the woods. This girl, blue with cold, greets Morozko with curses. The next day, instead of riches, the mother is horrified when she finds only her daughter's frozen, lifeless body. The moral of the tale: respect, don't curse, Old Man Winter. Of course, the brewers at Southern Tier might've thawed out that poor girl with a pint of this exceptionally hoppy old ale. Then everyone would've lived happily ever after.

❅ • ❅ • ❅ • ❅ • ❅ • ❅ • ❅ • ❅ • ❅ • ❅ • ❅ • ❅ • ❅ • ❅ • ❅ • ❅ • ❅

Originally, old ale was beer that had been aged a year or two. These days, old ale is another term for strong ale that is well hopped and malty, with a sherrylike finish.

46. 't Smisje Kerst

Brouwerij De Regenboog
Assebroek-Brugge, Belgium
No website
Style: **STRONG DARK ALE**
Alcohol volume: 11%
Serve with: Black Forest cake

I cannot even pretend to pronounce the name of this beer until I've consumed at least two bottles. Then, miraculously, I can speak fluent Flemish. Translated, it means "the Blacksmith Christmas," which summons images of tiny elves hammering away at shoes for the reindeer's hooves. In fact, Smisje is the name of the bus stop near brewer Johan Brandt's home; his neighbor's house was once a smith. Brandt's De Regenboog (Dutch for "rainbow") brewery is a small operation that produces tiny batches of oddly compelling ales flavored with the likes of mustard, raisins, and calvados. Kerst is made with coriander and grains of paradise, a West African spice that looks like peppercorn but, in addition to the heat, tastes of nuts and citrus. The beer is fruity, just as you'd expect from a strong Belgian ale, but with a hint of sourness. And then there's all that alcohol. Drink more than two, and you'll be positively *zatlap*.

❅ • ❅ • ❅ • ❅ • ❅ • ❅ • ❅ • ❅ • ❅ • ❅ • ❅ • ❅ • ❅ • ❅ • ❅ • ❅ • ❅

Just forty miles south of the De Regenboog brewery, in Ypres, is the site of one the
most powerful evocations of the holiday spirit: the Christmas Truce of 1914.
In the midst of unrelenting trench warfare along the Western Front during World War I,
German and British soldiers laid down their arms and celebrated the holiday by
singing carols and praying with each other.

47. Young's Winter Warmer
Wells & Young's Brewing
Bedford, England
www.youngs.co.uk
Style: **WINTER WARMER**
Alcohol volume: 5%
Serve with: Beef stew

The British tradition gave the world colonial rule, soggy fish and chips, soccer hooligans, and warm beer. Well, one out of four ain't bad—especially when you realize that warm beer, also known as cask ale, isn't really warm. Instead, it gets its name for the process in which the final stage of fermentation takes place inside a cask, properly stored in cool cellar temperatures. Bubbling along for weeks, it produces its own carbonation for a fresh, exceedingly smooth quaff. The style would have disappeared amid modernization in the 1970s if not for a beer-drinking lobby called the Campaign for Real Ale and tradition-bound breweries like Young's, which traces its roots to sixteenth-century Elizabethan England. Young's Winter Warmer is a satisfying fruity ale that is a British original. But for maximum enjoyment, you need to taste this beer as it was meant to be served, pulled with an old-fashioned hand pump from a subterranean cask at a London pub that's decorated for the holiday season.

❆ · ❆ · ❆ · ❆ · ❆ · ❆ · ❆ · ❆ · ❆ · ❆ · ❆ · ❆ · ❆ · ❆ · ❆ · ❆ · ❆ · ❆ · ❆

Young's also brews Christmas Pudding Ale, a brown ale with dried fruit flavor.

48. Snow Cap

Pyramid Breweries
Seattle, Washington
www.pyramidbrew.com
Style: **WINTER WARMER**
Alcohol volume: 7%
Serve with: Smoked salmon

As global warming continues, will those familiar snowcaps atop the mountains surrounding Seattle—the ones for which this ale is named—eventually disappear? Almost certainly. Not long ago, a University of Washington computer model estimated that temperatures in the Cascades and Olympic mountains will rise by 10 degrees before the end of this century. Their snow pack would be reduced to about 20 percent of their current levels. Less snow means even warmer temperatures and faster water runoff, which could lead to water shortages. And then there's the aesthetic damage. Snow, after all, is a necessary attribute of Christmas, what with Santa's sleigh and all. Snow Cap—a full-bodied ale with fruity undertones—won't melt away your environmental concerns. But at 7 percent alcohol, it's a true winter warmer, not a warmer winter.

❄ · ❄ · ❄ · ❄ · ❄ · ❄ · ❄ · ❄ · ❄ · ❄ · ❄ · ❄ · ❄ · ❄ · ❄ · ❄ · ❄ · ❄ · ❄

Snow Cap, one of the earliest American holiday craft beers, was originally brewed as a strong barleywine ale.

49. Nutcracker Ale

Boulevard Brewing
Kansas City, Missouri
www.blvdbeer.com
Style: **WINTER WARMER**
Alcohol volume: 6.1%
Serve with: Turkey kielbasa

Among the vast number of reasons beer is superior to wine is that it can be made year-round. No need to wait for grapes to grow and ripen to enjoy a glass: all of beer's ingredients can be dried and stored for months, allowing brewers to make (and enjoy) their product at a leisurely pace. For example, hop flowers, the plant that beer makers have used for centuries to bitter and balance their beers, are typically dried after they're picked; sometimes they are compacted into pellets or reduced to a liquid extract. Nutcracker Ale is an exceptional example of a new, and somewhat odd, trend in brewing: wet hops. They're fresh Chinook hops from Oregon that are rushed hundreds of miles to Kansas City within hours of harvest and added in the final stage of brewing to enhance its aroma and provide a spicy snap to its finish. Much as I enjoy the flavor, is this a trend that brewers really want to embrace? Guys, it's Christmastime—relax!

❅ · ❅ · ❅ · ❅ · ❅ · ❅ · ❅ · ❅ · ❅ · ❅ · ❅ · ❅ · ❅ · ❅ · ❅ · ❅ · ❅ · ❅ · ❅

Though Boulevard is the second biggest brewery in Missouri (behind you-know-who in St. Louis), its beer is available only in the Midwest.

50. Mönchshof Weihnachtsbier

Kulmbacher Brauerei

Kulmbach, Germany

www.kulmbacher.de

Style: **MARZEN**

Alcohol volume: 5.6%

Serve with: Dresden Christmas loaf
(bread with dried fruit)

It was the Sumerians of ancient Mesopotamia, according to historians, who discovered how to make beer about 4000 BC. If it wasn't for the spread of Islam, a religion that does not condone alcohol, the people of the Middle East would probably still be brewing in honor of Ninkasi, the goddess of brewing. Instead, it is Kulmbach, in the northern reaches of Bavaria, that can lay claim as the longest uninterrupted brewing region in the world. The evidence: an eighth-century-BC crock, unearthed at a burial site, that had been used to ferment beer. Over the next three millennia, the region became famous for a variety of unique beer styles, including bock, dark lager, and black beer. Mönchshof (monks' house) refers to the monastery where beer was brewed by Augustine monks as early as 1349. Today the brewery's Christmas treat, a malty, golden-orange lager, is made by the Kulmbach Brewing conglomerate.

Frohe Weihnachten *is German for "Merry Christmas."*

More Beers to Enjoy for Christmas

Aass Juleøl

Aass Brewery

Drammen, Norway

www.aass.no

Style: **DUNKEL BOCK**

Alcohol volume: 6.2%

Founded in 1834, Aass is Norway's
oldest brewery.

Abita Christmas Ale

Abita Brewing

Abita Springs, Louisiana

www.abita.com

Style: **AMBER ALE**

Alcohol volume: Varies

The recipe changes annually.

Ægir Julebrygg

Ægir Bryggeri

Flåm, Norway

www.aegirbryggeri.no

Style: **SPICED WINTER WARMER**

Alcohol volume: 4.7%

Ægir is one of the most beautiful
   brewpubs in the world. It is modeled
   after an ancient Norwegian stave
   church and is located alongside a
   scenic fjord.

Allagash Grand Cru

Allagash Brewing

Portland, Maine

www.allagash.com

Style: **BELGIAN STRONG PALE ALE**

Alcohol volume: 7.2%

With a fruit-and-spice aroma, this pairs
   nicely with Maine lobster.

Atwater Winter Bock

Atwater Block Brewery

Detroit, Michigan

www.atwaterbeer.com

Style: **BOCK**

Alcohol volume: 7.5%

A classic bock from a brewery with a
strong German heritage.

Bad Elf

Ridgeway Brewing

South Stoke, England

No Web site

Style: **INDIA PALE ALE**

Alcohol volume: 6%

A mildly hopped English-style IPA.

Bah Humbug

Wychwood Brewery

Witney, England

www.wychwood.co.uk

Style: **WINTER WARMER**

Alcohol volume: 6%

Is Bah Humbug too much of a downer?
Wychwood's sister brewery,
Brakspear, crafts a winter warmer
that is its spiritual opposite:
'O' Be Joyful.

Belgian Frostbite

River Horse Brewing

Lambertville, New Jersey

www.riverhorse.com

Style: **BELGIAN STRONG DARK ALE**

Alcohol volume: 8%

Brewed in a former oyster
cracker factory.

Big Shot

Fort Collins Brewery

Fort Collins, Colorado

www.fortcollinsbrewery.com

Style: **BROWN ALE**

Alcohol volume: 6.5%

Spiced with hazelnut.

Bink Winterkoninkske

Brouwerij Kerkom

Sint-Truiden, Belgium

www.brouwerijkerkom.be

Style: **BELGIAN STRONG DARK ALE**

Alcohol volume: 8.3%

Brewed with seven different malts,
    including rolled oats.

Blue Point Winter Ale

Blue Point Brewing

Patchogue, New York

www.bluepointbrewing.com

Style: **AMBER ALE**

Alcohol volume: 4.5%

Blue Point's brewery is housed in a
former ice factory.

Brooklyn Winter Ale

Brooklyn Brewery

Brooklyn, New York

www.brooklynbrewery.com

Style: **SCOTTISH ALE**

Alcohol volume: 6%

An alternate winter pick from the
brewery: Black Chocolate Stout.

Brown Shugga'

Lagunitas Brewing

Petaluma, California

www.lagunitas.com

Style: **BARLEYWINE**

Alcohol volume: 9.9%

- A dose of brown sugar helps spike the alcohol.

Criminally Bad Elf

Ridgeway Brewing

South Stoke, England

No Web site

Style: **BARLEYWINE**

Alcohol volume: 10.5%

Very malty, with subdued hops.

Cuvée Meilleurs Voeux

La Brasserie Artisanale de Rulles
Rulles, Belgium
www.larulles.be
Style: **BELGIAN STRONG DARK ALE**
Alcohol volume: 7.3%
Produced by a small brewery built
  in an old barn, this beer's name
  means "Best Wishes."

Dahls Juleøl

E. C. Dahls Brewery
Trondheim, Norway
No Web site
Style: **VIENNA LAGER**
Alcohol volume: 4.5%
Dahls also makes a stronger version
  of this lager at 6.3 percent alcohol,
  available only at Norway's wine
  monopoly stores.

Dominion Winter Brew

Old Dominion Brewing

Ashburn, Virginia

www.olddominion.com

Style: **INDIA PALE ALE**

Alcohol volume: 6.6%

Visit the Old Dominion Brewhouse at
the Washington, D.C., Convention
Center for an even fresher taste of
this holiday ale.

JW Dundee's Special Edition Festive Ale

High Falls Brewing

Rochester, New York

www.jwdundee.com

Style: **SPICED WINTER WARMER**

Alcohol volume: 6.2%

From the former Genesee brewery.

Faust Winter Festbier

Brauhaus Faust-Miltenberger

Miltenberg, Germany

www.faust.de

Style: **MARZEN**

Alcohol volume: 5.5%

Miltenberg is an exceptionally scenic medieval village. If you get the chance to visit, enjoy Faust beers at Gasthaus zum Riesen, which claims to be the oldest tavern in Germany (dating to the twelfth century).

Fish Tale WinterFish

Fish Brewing

Olympia, Washington

www.fishbrewing.com

Style: **DOUBLE IPA**

Alcohol volume: 7%

Exceptionally hopped with Yakima Chinook hops.

Föroya Bjór Jola Bryggj

Föroya Bjór

Klakksvík, Faroe Islands

www.foroya-bjor.fo

Style: **AMBER LAGER**

Alcohol volume: 5.4%

Also look for Jólaöl, a sweet, low-
alcohol Christmas beer.

Full Sail Wassail

Full Sail Brewing

Hood River, Oregon

www.fullsailbrewing.com

Style: **WINTER WARMER**

Alcohol volume: 6.5%

No spice in this wassail, just lots
of hops.

Fürst Carl Weihnachtsbock

Fürstliches Brauhaus Ellingen

Mittelfranken, Germany

www.fuerst-carl.de

Style: **DOUBLE BOCK**

Alcohol volume: 7.5%

Brewed at Bavaria's scenic
    Ellingen castle.

George Gale Christmas Ale

George Gale & Company

Horndean, England

www.gales.co.uk

Style: **WINTER WARMER**

Alcohol volume: 8.5%

Corked and suitable for aging.

Grand Cru Winter Reserve

Flying Fish Brewing

Cherry Hill, New Jersey

www.flyingfish.com

Style: **BELGIAN STRONG PALE ALE**

Alcohol volume: 7.2%

Grand cru is French for "great growth,"
a designation for a vineyard with a
very good reputation.

In the beer world, it simply means
"the very best."

Grinnin' Grizzly

Appalachian Brewing

Harrisburg, Pennsylvania

www.abcbrew.com

Style: **SPICED WINTER WARMER**

Alcohol volume: 4.5%

A foamy pint that tastes like a slice
of pumpkin pie.

Great Lakes Christmas Ale

Great Lakes Brewing

Cleveland, Ohio

www.greatlakesbrewing.com

Style: **SPICED WINTER WARMER**

Alcohol volume: 7.5%

Flavored with cinnamon, nutmeg, and honey.

Hacker-Pschorr Superior

Hacker-Pschorr Bräu

Munich, Germany

www.hacker-pschorr.de

Style: **HELLES**

Alcohol volume: 6%

Best enjoyed while shopping at Munich's Christkindlmarkt on its famous Marienplatz.

Hale's Ales Wee Heavy Winter Ale

Hale's Ales Brewery and Pub

Seattle, Washington

www.halesales.com

Style: **WEE HEAVY**

Alcohol volume: 7.2%

The authentic double-decker bus parked outside the brewery is the tip-off that Hale's is an English-style ale brewery.

Harpoon Winter Warmer

Harpoon Brewery

Boston, Massachusetts

www.harpoonbrewery.com

Style: **SPICED WINTER WARMER**

Alcohol volume: 5.5%

Harpoon staffers organize a huge annual volunteer effort throughout New England to decorate homeless centers each Christmas.

Harvey's Christmas Ale

Harveys Brewery

Lewes, England

www.harveys.org.uk

Style: **BARLEYWINE**

Alcohol volume: 8.2%

This strong ale is blessed by the local parish vicar.

He'brew Jewbelation

Shmaltz Brewing

San Francisco, California

www.shmaltz.com

Style: **DOUBLE IPA**

Alcohol volume: 11%

Shmaltz has notched up the alcohol by 1 percent in each year it has brewed this ale.

Herforder Weihnacht

Herforder Brauerei

Herford, Germany

www.herforder.de

Style: **MARZEN**

Alcohol volume: 5.8%

Light, malty, and crisp.

Hofbräu Festbier

Hofbräu München

Munich, Germany

www.hofbraeuhaus.de

Style: **MARZEN**

Alcohol volume: 6%

Warning to tourists visiting the famous
Hofbräuhaus: don't sit at a table
marked with a brass or wooden
plaque. It's a *Stammtisch*, or a table
for the regulars.

Hoppy Holidaze Flavored Ale

Marin Brewing

Larkspur, California

www.marinbrewing.com

Style: **SPICED WINTER WARMER**

Alcohol volume: 7%

Flavored with nutmeg, mace, cinnamon, vanilla, and orange peel.

Isolation Ale

Odell Brewing

Fort Collins, Colorado

www.odells.com

Style: **WINTER WARMER**

Alcohol volume: 6%

Warm and bracing, with a distinctive malt aroma.

K-9 Cruiser

Flying Dog Brewery

Denver, Colorado

www.flyingdogales.com

Style: **WINTER WARMER**

Alcohol volume: 6.4%

This brewery's labels boast the distinctive art of Ralph Steadman.

Kerstmutske Christmas Nightcap

Brouwerij Slaapmutske (at De Proef
Brewery)

Melle, Belgium

www.slaapmutske.be/

Style: **BELGIAN STRONG DARK ALE**

Alcohol volume: 7.4%

Slaapmutske is Flemish for "sleeping
cap" and slang for the last drink
before bed.

Klaster Winter Lager

Pivovar Klaster

Hradiste nad Jizerou, Czech Republic

www.klaster.com

Style: **AMBER LAGER**

Alcohol volume: 5.8%

Klaster ages its beer in a cave.

Klein Duimpje Kerstbier

Huisbrouwerij Klein Duimpje

Hillegom, the Netherlands

www.kleinduimpje.nl

Style: **BELGIAN STRONG DARK ALE**

Alcohol volume: 7.5%

Klein Duimpje is Dutch for
    "Tom Thumb."

König Ludwig Festtags-Bier

Schlossbrauerei Kaltenberg

Fürstenfeldbruck, Germany

www.kaltenberg.de

Style: **MARZEN**

Alcohol volume: 5.6%

Kaltenberg brewery is operated by a
   Bavarian prince.

La Moneuse Special Winter Ale

Brasserie de Blaugies

Blaugies, Belgium

www.brasseriedeblaugies.com

Style: **BELGIAN STRONG PALE ALE**

Alcohol volume: 8%

Formerly known as Spéciale Noël.

Lakefront Holiday Spice

Lakefront Brewery

Milwaukee, Wisconsin

www.lakefrontbrewery.com

Style: **SPICED WINTER WARMER**

Alcohol volume: 9.5%

The fruitcake of beers, flavored
  with cinnamon, orange zest, clove,
  and honey.

Lancaster Winter Warmer

Lancaster Brewing

Lancaster, Pennsylvania

www.lancasterbrewing.com

Style: **OLD ALE**

Alcohol volume: 8.9%

Lancaster was settled largely by
  Germans and in the mid-1800s
  was known as the Munich of the
  United States.

Lump of Coal

Ridgeway Brewing

South Stoke, England

No Web site

Style: **STOUT**

Alcohol volume: 8%

Strong, dark, and utterly enjoyable.

Mack Juleøl

Mack Bryggeri

Tromsø, Norway

www.mack.no

Style: **VIENNA LAGER**

Alcohol volume: 6.5%

At 250 miles inside the Arctic Circle,
Tromsø is home to the world's
northernmost production brewery.

Meckatzer Fest-Märzen

Meckatzer Löwenbräu

Heimenkirch, Germany

www.meckatzer.de

Style: **VIENNA LAGER**

Alcohol volume: 5.4%

A surprisingly well-hopped version
of this style.

Michelob Celebrate

Anheuser-Busch

St. Louis, Missouri

www.anheuser-busch.com

Style: **FRUIT BEER**

Alcohol volume: 8.5%

Flavored with cherries. Michelob also
brews a chocolate-flavored variety.

Never Summer Ale

Boulder Beer

Boulder, Colorado

www.boulderbeer.com

Style: **SPICED WINTER WARMER**

Alcohol volume: 5.9%

The brewer's not saying what spices he
adds. No matter—hops are the star
of this ale.

N'ice Chouffe

Brasserie d'Achouffe

Achouffe, Belgium

www.achouffe.be

Style: **BELGIAN STRONG DARK ALE**

Alcohol volume: 10%

Spiced with thyme and vanilla.

Nissemor

Haand Bryggeriet

Drammen, Norway

www.haandbryggeriet.net

Style: **OLD ALE**

Alcohol volume: 6%

Nissemor means "Mother Christmas"
in Norwegian. Brewed with raisins.

Noel de Calabaza

Jolly Pumpkin Artisan Ales

Dexter, Michigan

www.jollypumpkin.com

Style: **BELGIAN STRONG DARK ALE**

Alcohol volume: 9%

Exceptionally complex flavors of
caramel, nut, chocolate, and fruit,
aged in oak.

Nøgne Ø Winter Ale (God Jul)

Nøgne Ø Bryggeri

Grimstad, Norway

www.nogne-o.com

Style: **STOUT**

Alcohol volume: 8.5%

Nøgne Ø is Norwegian for "naked island."

Old Red Nose

Heartland Brewery

New York, New York

www.heartlandbrewery.com

Style: **SPICED WINTER WARMER**

Alcohol volume: 5.5%

Available in bottles or on tap only at Heartland's six New York locations.

Otter Creek Winter Ale

Otter Creek

Middlebury, Vermont

www.ottercreekbrewing.com

Style: **BROWN ALE**

Alcohol volume: 5.8%

Flavored with raspberry.

Prelude Special Ale

Shipyard Brewing

Portland, Maine

www.shipyard.com

Style: **WINTER WARMER**

Alcohol volume: 6.8%

The name comes from the Kenne-
bunkport Prelude, a ten-day
Christmas festival featuring a
parade, a Christmas tree decorated
with lobster buoys, and the arrival
of Santa on a motorboat.

Pursuit of Happiness

Clay Pipe Brewing

Westminster, Maryland

www.cpbrewing.com

Style: **WINTER WARMER**

Alcohol volume: 8.25%

Brewer Gregg Norris left a giant
Budweiser plant to start up this
microbrewery.

Ramstein Winter Wheat

High Point Brewing

Butler, New Jersey

www.ramsteinbeer.com

Style: **WEIZENBOCK**

Alcohol volume: 9.5%

High Point is America's first all-wheat
brewery.

The Raven Christmas Lager

Baltimore-Washington Beer Works

Nagold, Germany

www.ravenbeer.com

Style: **AMBER LAGER**

Alcohol volume: 5.5%

You have to travel all the way to Germany to buy this Baltimore beer, made under license by Anker-Brauerei for European beer drinkers.

Roxy Rolles

Magic Hat Brewing

Burlington, Vermont

www.magichat.net

Style: **AMBER ALE**

Alcohol volume: 5.8%

Look for it in Magic Hat's Feast of Fools twelve-pack.

Rude Elf's Reserve

Bethlehem Brew Works (at Weyer-
    bacher Brewing)

Bethlehem, Pennsylvania

www.thebrewworks.com

Style: **SPICED BELGIAN STRONG
    DARK ALE**

Alcohol volume: 10.5%

Spiced with cinnamon, nutmeg, sweet
    gale, cloves, coriander, and allspice.

Rudolph's Revenge

Cropton Brewery

Cropton, England

www.croptonbrewery.com

Style: **EXTRA SPECIAL BITTER**

Alcohol volume: 6%

Hoppy, with a fruity aftertaste.

Saint Arnold Christmas Ale

Saint Arnold Brewing

Houston, Texas

www.saintarnold.com

Style: **OLD ALE**

Alcohol volume: 7%

This brewery takes its name from St. Arnoldus of Metz, who once said: "From man's sweat and God's love, beer came into the world."

Samuel Adams Holiday Porter

Boston Beer

Boston, Massachusetts

www.samadams.com

Style: **PORTER**

Alcohol volume: 5.9%

Part of Sam Adams's holiday pack, which also includes a Cranberry Lambic and Old Fezziwig Ale.

Samuel Adams Winter Lager

Boston Beer

Boston, Massachusetts

www.samadams.com

Style: **WINTER WARMER**

Alcohol volume: 5.8%

An unusual hybrid lager made with
wheat and spices.

Santa's Butt

Ridgeway Brewing

South Stoke, England

no website

Style: **PORTER**

Alcohol volume: 6%

A *butt* is an old English keg measure.

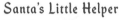

Santa's Little Helper

Mikkeller

Copenhagen, Denmark

www.mikkeller.dk

Style: **SPICED BELGIAN**
  STRONG DARK ALE

Alcohol volume: 11%

A deeply warming ale flavored with
  coriander and orange peel.

Santa's Little Helper

Port Brewing

San Marcos, California

www.portbrewing.com

Style: **IMPERIAL STOUT**

Alcohol volume: 10.5%

Also known as Santa's Little Hangover.

Saranac Chocolate Amber

Matt Brewing

Utica, New York

www.saranac.com

Style: **DARK LAGER**

Alcohol volume: 5.5%

It's not really made with chocolate—
   just dark chocolate malt.

Saranac Season's Best

Matt Brewing

Utica, New York

www.saranac.com

Style: **VIENNA LAGER**

Alcohol volume: 5.3%

An unusual mix of Belgian malts gives
   this a nutty flavor.

Saranac Winter Wassail

Matt Brewing

Utica, New York

www.saranac.com

Style: **SPICED WINTER WARMER**

Alcohol volume: 5.9%

Available in Saranac Twelve Beers of
   Winter packs.

Serafijn Christmas Angel

Microbrouweij Achilles

Itegem, Belgium

No Web site

Style: **BELGIAN STRONG PALE ALE**

Alcohol volume: 8%

Serafijn—or seraphim—is the highest
   rank of heavenly angels.

Sly Fox Christmas Ale

Sly Fox Brewing

Royersford, Pennsylvania

www.slyfoxbeer.com

Style: **SPICED WINTER WARMER**

Alcohol volume: 6.5%

Released each year on the eve of
    Thanksgiving.

SnowBound Winter Ale

Left Hand Brewing

Longmont, Colorado

www.lefthandbrewing.com

Style: **SPICED WINTER WARMER**

Alcohol volume: 7.6%

Left Hand Brewing founder Dick Doore
    got his start with a homebrewing kit
    he received as a Christmas present
    from his brother.

SnowStorm

August Schell Brewing

New Ulm, Minnesota

www.schellsbrewery.com

Style: **VARIES**

Alcohol volume: Varies

Both the recipe and the style change
  annually.

Sprecher Winter Brew

Sprecher Brewing

Glendale, Wisconsin

www.sprecherbrewery.com

Style: **BOCK**

Alcohol volume: 5.75%

This won a gold medal in the 2004
  World Beer Cup.

Stegmaier Holiday Warmer

The Lion Brewery

Wilkes-Barre, Pennsylvania

www.lionbrewery.com

Style: **WINTER WARMER**

Alcohol volume: 6.7%

Pours light, with a mild malt aroma.

Stoudt's Winter Ale

Stoudt's Brewing

Adamstown, Pennsylvania

www.stoudtsbeer.com

Style: **AMBER ALE**

Alcohol volume: 7%

The recipe changes every other year.

Summit Winter Ale

Summit Brewing

St. Paul, Minnesota

www.summitbrewing.com

Style: **WINTER WARMER**

Alcohol volume: 6.2%

An English-style ale, with an easy-to-drink body.

Thurn und Taxis Winter Festbier

Thurn und Taxis Brauerei

Regensburg, Germany

www.thurnundtaxisbiere.de

Style: **MARZEN**

Alcohol volume: 6%

The Thurn und Taxis palace in Regensburg houses a brewpub and hosts one of Bavaria's most impressive Christmas markets.

Tommyknocker Cocoa Porter

Tommyknocker Brewery

Idaho Springs, Colorado

www.tommyknocker.com

Style: **PORTER**

Alcohol volume: 5.7%

Brewed with cocoa beans and honey.

Tuborg Weihnachts Pilsener

Tuborg Bryggerier

Copenhagen, Denmark

www.tuborg.com

Style: **PILSNER**

Alcohol volume: 4.9%

Tuborg's German export. In Denmark,
the holiday pilsner, brewed to 5.7
percent alcohol, is called Julebryg.

Twelve Days

Hook Norton Brewery

Hook Norton, England

www.hooknortonbrewery.co.uk

Style: **BROWN ALE**

Alcohol volume: 5.5%

The Twelve Days of Christmas stretch
from Christmas Day to Epiphany
(January 6)

Very Bad Elf

Ridgeway Brewing

South Stoke, England

No Web site

Style: **EXTRA SPECIAL BITTER**

Alcohol volume: 7.5%

An amped-up version of Brakspear's
now-extinct Vintage Henley.

Vestfyen Julebryg

Bryggeriet Vestfyen

Assens, Denmark

www.bryggerietvestfyen.dk

Style: **MARZEN**

Alcohol volume: 5.7%

Also look for Vestfyen's Golden Christmas, a dark bock.

Viking Jólabjór

Vífilfell

Reykjavík, Iceland

www.vifilfell.is

Style: **AMBER LAGER**

Alcohol volume: 5.2%

Next to Christmas, the biggest drinking
celebration in Iceland is Beer Day on
March 1. It marks the date in 1989
when the country legalized beer.

Warm Welcome

Ridgeway Brewing

South Stoke, England

No Web site

Style: **BROWN ALE**

Alcohol volume: 6%

Bearing an image of Santa dangling over an open fire, this is a nut-browned ale. Get it?

Weeping Radish Christmas Beer

Weeping Radish Farm Brewery

Jarvisburg, North Carolina

www.weepingradish.com

Style: **DOUBLE BOCK**

Alcohol volume: 8%

Weeping Radish, North Carolina's oldest microbrewery, is located on an eco-farm that specializes in hormone-free beef.

Weyerbacher Winter Ale

Weyerbacher Brewing

Easton, Pennsylvania

www.weyerbacher.com

Style: **WINTER WARMER**

Alcohol volume: 5.6%

Need a stronger kick? Try Weyerbacher's Blithering Idiot barleywine.

White Christmas

Moylan's Brewery

Novato, California

www.moylans.com

Style: **BELGIAN WITBIER**

Alcohol volume: 6.5%

Brewer Brendan Moylan got his start
after buying, in his words, "the
Christmas gift I really wanted" —
a homebrewing kit.

Winter Cheer

Spanish Peaks Brewing

Denver, Colorado

www.blackdogales.com

Style: **AMBER ALE**

Alcohol volume: 6.3%

Copper colored, with a spicy
   hops finish.

Winter Koninck

Brouwerij De Koninck

Antwerp, Belgium

www.dekoninck.be

Style: **BELGIAN DARK ALE**

Alcohol volume: 6.5%

The left hand on the label is the brewery's symbol, taken from an old
   sculpted hand found on its original
   stone property-line post.

Winter Palace Wee Heavy

Paper City Brewery

Holyoke, Massachusetts

www.papercity.com

Style: **WEE HEAVY**

Alcohol volume: 8%

Smooth and full-bodied, with a sweet
malt finish.

Winterfest

Coors Brewing

Golden, Colorado

www.coors.com

Style: **AMBER ALE**

Alcohol volume: 5.6%

In 2007, Coors temporarily discontin-
ued this brand—one of America's
oldest mass-produced Christmas
beers. As of publication, there was
no word on its return.

Winter Hook

Red Hook

Woodinville, Washington, and

Portsmouth, New Hampshire

www.redhook.com

Style: **WINTER WARMER**

Alcohol volume: 5.5%

The recipe changes annually.

Winter's Bourbon Cask Ale

Anheuser-Busch

St. Louis, Missouri

www.anheuser-busch.com

Style: **SPICED WINTER WARMER**

Alcohol volume: 6%

Brewed with vanilla beans and aged in
oak casks.

Wizard's Winter Ale

Middle Ages Brewing

Syracuse, New York

www.middleagesbrewing.com

Style: **WINTER WARMER**

Alcohol volume: 6.8%

Brewed in a former ice cream plant.

Zinnebir X-Mas

Brasserie De La Senne

Sint-Pieters-Leeuw, Belgium

www.brasseriedelasenne.be

Style: **BELGIAN PALE ALE**

Alcohol volume: 6.6%

The dogs on the label are mutts
known in Belgium as *zinneke*,
or "little bastards."

Some Recipes and
Practical Info

Homemade Christmas Beer

Making your own beer is remarkably easy. Home-brew shops and mail-order suppliers can provide all the ingredients, materials, and advice that you need.

For the holidays, you'll want something special, and this full-flavored ale is just the ticket. The recipe is from George Hummel, who runs Home Sweet Homebrew in Philadelphia. He's adapted it from his recipe for George's Fault, a grand cru–style beer that won a gold medal at the Great American Beer Festival in 2005. Hummel calls it Sanity Claus.

Depending on your fermentation skills, you should reach about 10 to 12 percent alcohol with this beer. A glass, or three, should be just enough to test your sanity.

INGREDIENTS

Grains

- 1 pound Weyermann Carafoam
- 1 pound Weyermann CaraHelles

Malt extracts

- 8 pounds Alexander's Sun Country wheat malt extract
- 1¼ pounds Alexander's Sun Country pale malt extract

Kettle sugars

- 2 pounds orange-blossom honey
- 1 pound Home Sweet Homebrew
- Clear Belgian Rock Candy Sugar

Hops

- **2 ounces Styrian Aurora hops**

Spices

- **1 ounce Indian coriander seed**
- **1 ounce bitter orange peel**
- **1 ounce mandarin orange peel**
- **½ ounce chamomile**
- **¼ ounce grains of paradise**

Additives

- **2 teaspoons yeast nutrient**
- **1 teaspoon Irish moss**
- **1 Campden tablet**

Yeast

- **Wyeast No. 3522**

Priming sugar

- **5 ounces dextrose**

DIRECTIONS

Heat 6 gallons of water in a large pot to 175 degrees F. Add and dissolve the Campden tablet, maintain temperature, and let it rest for 15 minutes.

Coarsely crack the grains and submerge them in a cheesecloth bag in the brewing kettle. Let it rest for 30 minutes. Remove the grain bag and discard (sparge optional).

Heat to a boil. Add the pale malt extract and 1½ ounces of the hops to the kettle and dissolve. Boil for 45 minutes. Remove from heat. Add wheat malt extract and the kettle sugars and dissolve. Return to heat and boil.

Grind all the spices, place them in a cheesecloth bag, and add them to the kettle. Boil for an additional 15 minutes. Add the remaining hops and turn off the heat.

Follow normal fermentation and bottling procedures.

Brew 3 to 6 months in advance.

Eggnog

These days we add rum or brandy to eggnog, but in the original seventeenth-century British recipe, it was made with beer. Indeed, "nog" is an old English word for strong ale. Another thing: Until the invention of refrigeration in the late nineteenth century, eggnog was served warm.

Here's a recipe from Lucy Saunders, author of *The Best of American Beer and Food*. Use a malty and spicy Christmas beer, not one that's too hoppy or bitter. For a thicker nog, reduce the ale to 8 ounces.

INGREDIENTS

- 1 cup sugar
- 1 cup water
- 1 teaspoon vanilla
- ¼ cup raw honey
- 6 whole eggs, plus 1 egg white
- 2 cups heavy cream
- 12 ounces winter ale, at room temperature, decanted and whisked to remove carbonation
- ½ cup dark rum, or more to taste
- ¼ cup cognac or Cointreau
- 1 teaspoon cinnamon
- pinch ground cloves
- ¼ teaspoon allspice
- Fresh grated nutmeg to taste

DIRECTIONS

Mix sugar and water in a heavy 2-quart saucepan over high heat, stirring until dissolved. Let simmer until caramel colored, about 5 minutes, to make a simple syrup. Remove syrup from heat and stir in vanilla and honey. Using a stand mixer fitted with a wire whip, beat eggs on medium speed until frothy. Slowly drizzle a very thin thread of hot syrup into the egg blend, mixing constantly. Eggs will begin to turn fluffy and light yellow. (Do not pour all the syrup into the eggs at once, as the mixture will curdle.) Stop the mixer and scrape the sides of the bowl with a spatula to blend evenly.

Mix in other ingredients, one at a time. Be sure to use ale at room temperature, whisked and allowed to settle to remove carbonation. The ale will foam as it is mixed in. Add all the spices except grated nutmeg, and chill until very cold.

Whisk again before serving and for a perfectly smooth nog, pour it through a sieve. Taste and adjust the spices. Top each cup with freshly grated nutmeg.

Makes 8 servings.

NOG ON TAP

Norfolk Nog from Woodforde's brewery in England is a full-flavored favorite—without the eggs. It's a dark-ruby old ale with a coffee aroma and a hint of chocolate. In 1992, it was named the Supreme Champion Beer of Britain.

Biersuppe

In Germany, families hand down their recipes for this traditional Christmas soup from generation to generation. It's served either before Christmas dinner or as a late-night treat. You can add raisins, cinnamon, or other spices.

INGREDIENTS

- 6 cups beer
- 2 egg yolks
- 1 cup sour cream
- 1 teaspoon cornstarch
- 1 teaspoon white sugar
- ½ teaspoon salt
- ½ lemon (juice and grated rind)
- 4 slices French bread, cut into bite-size cubes
- 1 cup shredded Swiss cheese

DIRECTIONS

Pour beer into saucepan and allow it to rest until it's flat, about 2 hours. Cover and bring to a light boil over medium heat (be careful not to boil over). In a bowl, beat together egg yolks, sour cream, cornstarch, sugar, salt, and lemon juice and rind. Pour into saucepan with beer and lower heat. Simmer about 20 minutes.

Place bread cubes in soup bowls, sprinkle with cheese, and cover with soup.

Serves four.

Beer-Can Turkey

You know that crazy recipe for beer-can chicken on your grill? You can adapt it quite easily for a succulent turkey dinner on Christmas Day. Don't scrimp on the beer, either. Using your favorite holiday brews adds to the flavor.

The hard part of this recipe is keeping the bird upright. Instead of balancing it on a tiny 12-ounce can, pour your beer into an emptied, heavy-gauge sided 24-ounce soup can. Trim away any bone until the can fits completely inside the bird. Then place the bird, standing upright, in a roasting pan.

If you're worried about a mess, you can also simply place the turkey on a roasting rack and fill the drip pan with the beer.

For the moistest meat, brine the turkey in a salt-and-sugar solution the night before cooking.

INGREDIENTS

- 1 whole turkey (15–20 pounds)
- 4 tablespoons paprika
- 2 tablespoons onion powder
- 2 tablespoons garlic powder
- 3 tablespoons dried thyme leaves
- 1 tablespoon ground cumin
- 1 tablespoon cayenne pepper
- ½ cup sugar
- 1 cup salt
- ¼ cup canola oil
- 18 ounces spiced Christmas beer

DIRECTIONS

Preheat oven to 350 degrees F.

Remove giblets and neck from turkey. Rinse with cold water and thoroughly pat dry.

In a small bowl, combine spices and herbs for rub. Brush turkey with oil. Rub interior of bird with 2–3 teaspoons of spice mixture, then cover exterior, remembering to spread the rub beneath the skin.

Fill a can with beer and lift the bird onto the can. (As an alternative, place the turkey on a roasting rack in a large pan, and fill the pan with beer.)

Roast for about 4 to 5 hours, until juices are clear. The interior temperature of the breast meat should be 170 degrees F.

When removing turkey from the oven, be careful not to spill the beer. (And don't be tempted to drink it, either!)

Let rest 20 minutes before carving. Serve warm.

St. Martin's Goose

Beer expert Horst Dornbusch shares this story, and recipe, of an old-time favorite that is still served throughout Germany.

The fourth-century son of a Roman tribune born in what is now Hungary, St. Martin of Tours chose a life a godliness, quitting the military to become a priest. When the Church attempted to make him a bishop, legend says that Martin tried to hide in a goose pen. The noisy birds gave him away, though, and Martin served as a reluctant but beloved bishop until his death on November 11.

To this day, people bake a goose on the anniversary, exacting mock revenge on the traitorous birds. As it happens, November 11 is also the opening of bock season in Germany, with the first malty festbiers making their appearance.

INGREDIENTS

- 1 goose (12 – 16 pounds)
- salt and black pepper
- mugwort and/or marjoram
- 2 apples (1 sweet and 1 sour variety)
- parsley (optional)
- 1 onion
- beer for basting (preferably a malty one, like altbier or bockbier)

DIRECTIONS

Rub the goose inside and out with salt and pepper. Rub the inside with mugwort (and/or marjoram).

Dice the apples and the onion, as well as the optional parsley, and combine. Stuff the goose with the mixture. Close the goose openings with skewers.

Bake at 400 degrees F, breast down, for one-third of the total baking time. Turn bird on one side and bake for one-sixth of the total time. Turn bird on the other side for another one-sixth of the total. Turn bird on back for one-third of the total time to crisp the breasts.

Prick skin often to render the fat and baste frequently with beer to keep moist.

Calculate about 2 pounds per person. Total baking time is about 25 minutes per pound (or about 6 hours for a 14-pound bird).

Bier Fisch

Carp is the favored fish for this classic German Christmas dish. In America, try using a whole sea bass.

INGREDIENTS

- 1 whole carp (2–3 pounds), cleaned
- 2 tablespoons butter
- 1 medium onion, chopped
- 1 stalk celery
- 3 cloves garlic, peeled
- ½ teaspoon salt
- ½ teaspoon pepper
- 4 lemon slices
- 1 bay leaf
- 1 bottle festbier
- 6 Pfeffernüsse cookies or gingersnaps, crushed
- ¼ cup frozen raspberries
- 1 tablespoon sugar
- salt
- fresh parsley

DIRECTIONS

Clean and gut fish, leaving bones, and remove the head and salt the fish lightly. Let stand for 30 minutes.

Melt butter in a large skillet, then lightly sauté onion, celery, and garlic, adding salt and pepper. Lay fish in pan, add lemons and bay leaf. Gently pour beer into pan. Simmer for 15 minutes, until the fish flakes.

Remove fish and cover to keep warm.

Strain liquid through sieve, pressing vegetables to extract the juice. Return liquid to skillet and add cookies, raspberries, and sugar, stirring until thickened. Pour sauce over fish, and garnish with parsley.

Cranberry Wit Sauce

This is a traditional holiday side dish with a twist, from Sean Z. Paxton of *Beer Advocate* magazine.

INGREDIENTS

- 2 blood oranges, zested and sliced into rings
- 2 cups witbier
- ½ cup Belgian clear rock candy sugar, or regular sugar
- 2 teaspoons ground coriander
- pinch sea salt
- ½ cup orange blossom honey
- 12 ounces fresh cranberries

DIRECTIONS

In a large saucepan, add oranges, giving a good twist to release the juice (reserve the zest), witbier, rock candy, coriander, and salt. Bring to a boil over medium-high heat, stirring about 4 minutes until the sugar has dissolved. Remove the oranges and add the honey, orange zest, and cranberries; reduce the heat to medium-low and simmer until the cranberries have popped and the sauce has thickened, about 15 minutes. Serve immediately. The sauce can be made up to 2 days in advance.

Wassail

Whether you're entertaining guests or warming up carolers, a large bowl of wassail is a welcome treat. The secret of mulled beer is freshly ground spices. Instead of sprinkling them from a jar that's been sitting in your spice rack for the past year, use whole spices. Grind cinnamon sticks and whole nutmeg into your bowl. Take whole cloves or coriander seeds and mash them with a mortar and pestle. And never use ginger powder; instead, grate directly from a ginger root. For added flavor, gently preroast the spices in a skillet.

Here's a basic recipe that will make enough for a good-sized party.

INGREDIENTS

- 12 small baking apples
- 12 12-ounce bottles of Christmas beer or ale
- 1 cup firmly packed brown sugar
- 4 cinnamon sticks
- 2 teaspoons whole cloves
- 1 teaspoon ground ginger
- 8 whole allspice
- pinch nutmeg
- 2 4-inch strips orange peel (remove white pith)
- 4 cups cream sherry

DIRECTIONS

Bake apples whole in a shallow pan for 20 minutes at 375 degrees F.

Pour 3 bottles of the beer into a large stock pot and add the sugar, spices, and orange peel. Simmer over low heat for 10 minutes.

Gradually add about 6 more bottles of beer plus the sherry. Bring to a boil, then lower the heat and simmer for 5 more minutes.

Add the last 3 bottles of beer and heat for 30 seconds.

Pour into a punch bowl with as many apples as will fit, or serve from the pan with the apples floating on top.

THE WASSAIL BOWL OF YULETIDE

Pour a quart of good ale into a preserving pan with a pint of elder (this is optional but if omitted add a little more ale), four ounces sugar, and about a spoonful of pounded cloves; stir it over the fire until the sugar is all melted, and the ale, etc., is all but boiling. Roast four or five apples (they should be crabs, but common ones are very good), lay them in the wassail bowl, sprinkle them with about a teaspoonful of mixed spice, pour on them the hot beer, slip in two or three slices of lemon, and serve.

—From the Edwardsville (Illinois) *Intelligencer*, 1891

A CAROUSING ALE

"The drinking of the wassail bowl was, in all probability, owing to keeping Christmas in the same manner they had before the Feast of Yule. There was nothing the Northern nations so much delighted in as carousing ale, especially at this season when fighting was over. It was likewise the custom at their feasts for the master of the house to fill a large bowl or pitcher and drink out of it first himself, and then give it to him that sat next, and so it went round."

—*The Gentleman's Magazine*, 1784

BREAKFAST OF CHAMPIONS

In the seventeenth century, university students celebrated Christmas with a stomach-turning concoction called Flip. Here's the recipe, from *In Praise of Ale: Songs, Ballads, Epigrams and Anecdotes Relating to Beer* by W. T. Marchant, 1888.

Add lemon juice and cinnamon to one quart of strong home-brewed beer, bring to a boil in a saucepan, then add one glass of gin. In a separate dish, beat 8 egg yolks with sugar and grated nutmeg. Pour beer mixture onto eggs, then drink—if you dare.

Pfeffernüsse

These hard German cookies are traditionally dunked into steaming cups of hot mulled wine. But you can try them with beer, too. The recipe is courtesy of Susan J. Talbott of Christmas-Baking.com.

INGREDIENTS

- 2 eggs
- 1½ cups sugar
- ¼ cup candied ginger, citron, or orange, finely chopped
- ⅓ cup almonds, ground
- zest of ½ lemon or ½ teaspoon lemon extract
- 2½ cups flour
- 1 teaspoon baking powder
- 1 teaspoon cinnamon
- ½ teaspoon ground cloves
- ½ teaspoon ground cardamom
- ½ teaspoon ground ginger
- ¼ teaspoon pepper
- ¼ cup milk

Glaze:

- 1½ cups powdered sugar
- juice of half a lemon

DIRECTIONS

Beat eggs and sugar together at high speed in a mixer until tripled in volume and very pale, about 3 to 5 minutes. Add crystalized ginger (or citron), nuts, and lemon zest or extract to egg mixture and mix until combined. Change mixer to the paddle blade. Sift together flour, baking powder, and spices, and slowly add to the egg mixture. If the dough is dry and crumbly, add milk 1 tablespoon at a time until dough holds together. Knead gently for 1 to 2 minutes until the dough is smooth. Cover and let sit for 1 day unrefrigerated; this step is important to allow the flavors to meld.

The next day, preheat oven to 325 degrees F. Form dough into balls about 1 to 1½ inches in diameter; place on a parchment-covered baking sheet. Bake 20 to 25 minutes until browned. Allow to cool 20 minutes.

In a small bowl, whisk together powdered sugar and lemon juice (add a bit of hot water for a thinner glaze). Dip the tops of the cookies into the glaze and allow excess to drip off. (A cooling rack placed over the parchment-lined baking sheets works well.) Store in an airtight container.

Sugar Mama Pecans

Maybe you're not ready for a big meal, but you'll certainly need snacks to go with all this good beer. Here's a quick and easy treat from Carolyn Smagalski, the Beer Fox at Bella Online (www.bellaonline.com), that I've tweaked with a Christmas beer.

INGREDIENTS

- **4 tablespoons butter**
- **1½ cups firmly packed brown sugar**
- **4 ounces Sierra Nevada Celebration Ale**
- **½ teaspoon salt**
- **¼ teaspoon Tabasco sauce**
- **¼ teaspoon cinnamon**
- **2 pounds shelled pecans**

DIRECTIONS

Preheat oven to 350 degrees F.

In a small saucepan over low to medium heat, melt butter and brown sugar, stirring constantly. Add ale, salt, Tabasco sauce, and cinnamon. Stir in pecans and coat evenly.

Spread pecans in a single layer on a greased cookie sheet. Bake for 20 minutes. Watch pecans carefully—do not allow mixture to smoke or burn.

Cool in single layer on buttered waxed paper.

✁ COLLECT 'EM, DRINK 'EM ✁

Where can you find the great Christmas beers of the world?

While the likes of Coors, Anheuser-Busch, Anchor, and Sierra Nevada enjoy national distribution, most of the beers in this book are produced by either small American craft brewers or specialty beer makers overseas. Sadly, they do not benefit from wide distribution. Moreover, the oddities of U.S. beer laws prevent some distributors from sending their beer to certain states or counties. Although mail order regulations are easing across the country, few breweries will send you beer, even if you're willing to pay for costly shipping.

But you're a devoted beer drinker, right? None of this should dissuade you. Instead, grab your bottle opener and hit the road for your own seasonal beer hunt. The following are some of the best holiday beer festivals.

Belgian ecstasy

To get a taste of more than one hundred different Belgian Christmas ales, make your way to Essen, Belgium, near the Dutch border, for the annual two-day Kerstbierfestival. It's the best Christmas beer fest in the world, and it's worth the trip.

The event, organized by the very serious-sounding Objective Beer Tasters Essen Region (O.B.E.R.), presents nearly every Christmas beer bottled in Belgium in one cavernous meeting hall. Hundreds of visitors from around the world fill the place, looking for sips of Père Noël, Stille Nacht, La Moneuse Spéciale Noël, Corsendonk, Bush Prestige, St. Feuillien, and dozens more.

It's held on the second or third weekend of December. You can find more information at www.kerstbierfestival.be, or follow the news at the Burgundian Babblebelt (www.babblebelt.com), an Internet news group that shares information on the Belgian beer scene.

The great Northwest

In the United States, one of the biggest Christmas beer festivals is held annually in the cold, dark outdoors of Portland, Oregon. Under a clear tent in Pioneer Courthouse Square, more than three dozen robust winter ales are poured for shivering beer lovers at the annual Holiday Ale Festival. Portland is the self-proclaimed Beer Town of America, and this event shows why. Happy visitors sing along with Christmas music and fill their souvenir mugs with the likes of Blizzard of Oz, Liquid Cheer, Sled Crasher, and Tannen Bomb.

It's usually held on the first weekend of December. For information, go to www.holidayale.com or call 503-252-9899.

Vintage Second City

One of the widest selections of holiday beers in America can be found at the annual Christmas ale tasting at Delilah's in Chicago. On the second Saturday of December, owner Mike Miller hauls out more than one hundred different beers from around the world, including many that he's aged in his own cellar. Here you can sample a half dozen different vintages of Anchor Our Special Ale or Kings and Barnes from England. One of Miller's favorites: Belgian Fantome, circa 1998.

As a bonus, you can get some of your holiday shopping done at the same time. Local artisans set up tables in the bar and sell handcrafts and other gift items.

For information, go to www.delilahschicago.com or call 773-472-2771.

Toga!

Grab a bed sheet and head to the Saturnalia festival at the New Albanian Brewing Co., Pub & Pizzeria in New Albany, Indiana. The heathens raise many pints to Saturn, the Roman god of the harvest who started much of this fun, with casks of its own fine ales, plus dozens of other winter warmers from around the world. The kegs are tapped in a ritualistic ceremony on the first weekend of December, and the paganism begins.

For information, go to www.newalbanian.com or call 812-944-2577.

More places to sample holiday cheer

Scores of brewpubs and taverns across the country hold annual Christmas beer fests, often with a wide selection of ales and special menus. Here are a few notable places where you can enjoy the festivities, typically held in late November or early December.

THE BREWER'S ART MID-ATLANTIC CHRISTMAS BEER FESTIVAL. 1106 N. Charles St., Baltimore, Maryland. 410-547-6925. www.belgianbeer.com

CHANUKAH VS. CHRISTMAS, sponsored by Shmaltz Brewing, is held at several bars in major cities. The brewery matches up its He'brew "chosen beers" against the gentiles' brews. See www.shmaltz.com for locations and information.

ZENO'S PUB WINTER AND CHRISTMAS BEER FESTIVAL. 100 W. College Ave., State College, Pennsylvania. 814-237-2857. www.zenospub.com

BEER CORNER, U.S.A., HOLIDAY BEER FESTIVAL AT BEERTOPIA, HUBER HAUS, AND CRESCENT MOON. 36th and Farnam streets, Omaha, Nebraska. 402-345-1708. www.beercornerusa.com

CAPITAL ALE HOUSE KERSTBIER FEST (one of the top beer bars in America). 623 E. Main St., Richmond, Virginia. 804-780-ALES. www.capitalalehouse.com

WINTER BEER FESTIVAL, sponsored by the Washington Beer Commission. Hale's Brewery and Pub, 4301 Leary Way NW, Seattle, Washington. 206-706-1544. www.washingtonbeer.com

WINTERFEST, featuring Philadelphia-area holiday beers. General Lafayette Inn and Brewery, 646 Germantown Pike, Lafayette Hill, Pennsylvania. 610-941-0600. www.generallafayetteinn.com

Buying

Traveling over the holidays? Make sure you drop by a local shop to pick up a handful of regional holiday microbrews or a rare import. Many specialty stores will let you mix a sixpack, so you can enjoy a variety of flavors.

Here are some of the best beer stores in the United States:

BELMONT STATION. 4500 SE Stark St., Portland, Oregon. 503-232-8538. www.belmont-station.com

BIERKRAFT (online sales). 191 Fifth Ave., Brooklyn, New York. 718-230-7600. www.bierkraft.com

BOISE CO-OP. 888 W. Fort St., Boise, Idaho. 208-472-4500. www.boisecoop.com

BOTTLEWORKS. 1710 N. 45th St., Suite 3, Seattle, Washington. 206-633-2437. www.bottleworks.com

CHEVY CHASE WINE AND SPIRITS. 5544 Connecticut Ave. NW, Washington, D.C. 202-363-4000. www.chevychasewine.com

THE FOODERY. 324 S. 10th St. and 837 N. 2nd St., Philadelphia, Pennsylvania. 215-928-1111. www.fooderybeer.com

JOHN'S GROCERY. 401 E. Market St., Iowa City, Iowa. 319-337-2183. www.johnsgrocery.com

THE PARTY SOURCE. 95 Riviera Dr., Bellevue, Kentucky. 859-291-4007. www.thepartysource.com

PREMIER GOURMET (online sales). 3465 Delaware Ave., Buffalo, New York. 716-877-3574. www.premiergourmet.com

SAM'S WINE & SPIRITS (online sales). 1720 N. Marcey St., Chicago, Illinois. 800-777-9137. www.samswine.com

STATE LINE LIQUORS. 1610 Elkton Road, Elkton, Maryland. 800-446-9463. www.statelineliquors.com

TULLY'S BEER AND WINE. US Route 1, Hannaford Plaza, Wells, Maine. 207-641-8622. www.tullysbeerandwine.com

Serving Up a
❧ HOLIDAY BREW ❧

Don't go chugging that twenty-dollar corked bottle—Christmas beer deserves to be savored. The following are some general guidelines for optimum enjoyment of a special holiday brew.

Temperature

Americans like their beer cold, but frigid temperatures chill your taste buds and prevent you from appreciating the complex flavors of many ales and lagers. Typically, ales should be served at a temperature of about 50 degrees F, and even closer to 60 degrees F for barleywine and strong ale. So if you've pulled a bottle straight from the fridge, let it sit a half hour before opening. If the beer hasn't been cooled yet, stick it in a bucket with ice and water for about fifteen to twenty minutes.

Pouring

Beer was meant to foam. If you pour it all down the side of the glass, its carbonation won't be properly released and you'll be swallowing gas. Hold the glass at a 45-degree angle and pour slowly down the side. After the glass is one-third full, straighten it and pour the rest of the beer in the middle, raising the bottle smoothly.

A Belgian golden ale or saison will often produce a massive, pillowy head. That's part of its character.

Unfiltered beer often has a yeast bed at the bottom of the bottle. It's perfectly fine to drink (some say it contains healthy vitamins), but if you want to avoid pouring it into your glass, leave an ounce of beer in the bottle.

Glassware

Many breweries design specific glasses for their beers, available on the Internet or at specialty beer stores. For the beers in this book, you can get by with four basic designs:

BRITISH PINT. The straight-sided 16-ounce American version of this glass (often used as a mixing glass by bartenders) is boring and may not accommodate an entire beer plus head. Get the 20-ounce imperial pint with a bulbed top to handle the foam. Good for pale ale, light lager, porter, stout, India pale ale

GOBLET. Heavy and thick, this glass is made to hold a formidable beer—one whose head will rise to the rim and then settle in a laced pattern as you take each mighty quaff. Good for Belgian dubbel, Belgian tripel, strong dark ale

SNIFTER. The same glass typically used for single malt is ideal for strong beers that were made for sipping. Cup it in your hand and don't be afraid to let the ale warm to your body temperature. Raise it to your mouth and the aromas of alcohol, hops, and malt will waft to your nose. Good for barleywine, old ale, Scotch ale, imperial IPA

TULIP OR THISTLE. Shaped like a tulip petal, this form is designed to capture the foam while allowing you to stick your nose right into the aromatic pillow. Good for saison, bière de garde, Belgian golden ale

Tasting

'Tis the season to slow down and enjoy the scenery.

Use your eyes to examine the color, the body, the head.

Use your nose to appreciate the aroma. Remember, much of the taste is enhanced through your sense of smell.

Use your palate to savor the flavor. Sip and let the beer flood every part of your mouth. Consider how it tastes on the side of your tongue, how it feels on the inside of your cheeks. Breathe out and detect still more flavors.

And swallow! This is beer, not wine.

Cellaring

Despite everything you've heard about freshness dating and born-on dates, you don't chug many of the bottles in this book. While most lagers and pale ales are best consumed within six months, many Christmas beers can be stored for years. The reason? Hops and alcohol, two of the main ingredients in beer. In sufficient quantities, both act as preservatives.

Hoppy beers, like India pale ale and barleywine, can last a year, maybe two, if properly stored. High-alcohol beers, such as imperial stout and Belgian-style strong ales, last even longer, typically up to five years. Some beers are dated, so you can remember how long you've been holding onto that bottle.

In storing beer, the single most important precaution is to keep it out of the sunlight. Aside from oxygen, nothing spoils beer faster than light. If your bottles are stored in a room with windows, keep them in a cardboard box.

Secondly, maintain a consistent temperature. Some people go to all kinds of extremes to hold their bottles at a perfect 54 degrees F, but not all of us are so lucky to own thirty-five-thousand-dollar cedar-paneled, humidity-controlled cellars. Beer—especially high-alcohol beer—is not so delicate that you need to maintain a precise temperature. Just avoid huge temperature swings, like 90 degrees in the summer to 20 degrees in the winter. In other words, don't store all those carefully selected imported ales in your garage or attic. The fridge—especially one whose temperature can be set in the mid-50s—is fine. The best place for storing beer is a cellar. Keep the beer from direct contact with the floor, to prevent damage during flooding, washing-machine overflows, or other disasters. Stand the bottles upright. Most corked bottles don't need the added moisture that accrues from laying them on their sides. Plus, standing the bottles upright will keep the yeast sediment on the bottom, where it belongs.

Some people keep a ledger to record when they got which beer. I usually just date the cap with a Sharpie, so I know how long the bottle has been sitting.

Cellaring beer is not an exact science—some bottles go bad, some don't really improve. The fun is in discovering just how flavors mature and change with time. Often you'll find that hugely flavored ales mellow and become even more enjoyable with age. The bitterness of hops abates, allowing you to enjoy their gardenlike flavor. The sweetness softens, and more of the malt notes become evident. You might notice the aroma of sherry or almond, a product of oxidation. Unfiltered beer with live yeast in the bottle will continue to ferment, notching up the alcohol a half percent or so.

Oh, and one other reason for storing: there's nothing quite like pulling out a cellared Christmas beer to impress your friends or treat yourself to a holiday gift in the middle of July.

❧ STYLE NOTES ❧

Technically speaking, Christmas beer is not a style. Unlike brown ale or bock or pilsner, or any of the other scores of recognized beer styles, these seasonal delights can't be defined by color, alcohol content, or flavor.

Indeed, not all of the bottles in this book are called "Christmas" beer. In this secular age, many of them are euphemistically labeled "holiday" brews or "winter warmers." No big deal—we all know the truth: not one of them would be on the shelves if it weren't for Christmas.

Christmas beer—or winter warmer or holiday ale—is whatever the brewer says it is. Indeed, over the years, a brewery may change its style of Christmas beer completely, from a bitter pale ale to a sweet bock.

The only criteria is that the beer must be special. It must be produced specifically for the holiday season, and its packaging must reflect this.

That said, the Beer Judge Certification Program, whose style definitions are frequently cited as the final word on beer, does recognize a Christmas beer category:

> STYLE 21B—CHRISTMAS/WINTER SPECIALTY SPICED BEER: A stronger, darker, spiced beer that often has a rich body and warming finish, suggesting a good accompaniment for the cold winter season.

Although that accurately defines the likes of Anchor's Our Special Ale and Samuel Adams's Winter Lager, it surely does not include a raft of other popular Christmas beers, such as Sierra Nevada Celebration or Samichlaus.

So without an accurate style definition, how do you know what kind of Christmas beer you're drinking? Simple—by taste.

It may be obvious, but it's worth stating: flavor is the single most important factor in beer enjoyment. There is much more to appreciate. Pour the beer into a glass and take a sip—is it sweet, is it bitter? Examine the color. Is it dark or light? Is it bright or murky? Take a deep whiff of the aroma. Is it fruity or flowery? Consider its body. Is it light and bubbly, or full bodied and frothy? And most importantly, do you like it?

The thing to remember here is to give the beer a chance. Crack open a bottle without prejudging, and don't get caught up in style definitions. After all, it's Christmastime, and the beer is a gift from the brewer. Unwrap it with joy and smile. Sure, maybe it's a polka dot tie that you'll never wear again. But you wouldn't gripe about a gift from your Aunt Bertha, would you?

⛤ DEFINING BEER STYLES ⛤

Beer is generally divided into two categories, based on its method of fermentation. Ales are fermented at warmer temperatures for short periods with yeast that works from the top. This method tends to impart more distinct flavors that may be either fruity or spicy.

Lagers are fermented at cooler temperatures for longer periods with yeast that works at the bottom. Lagers tend to have a crisp, clean taste.

Within these two categories, there are dozens of styles and subcategories. The following are the styles reflected by popular Christmas beers.

Ale

AMBER, RED, OR DARK ALE. Flavorful and balanced, with low to moderate alcohol. Red ale is a bit toastier; Belgian dark ale is more complex.

BARLEYWINE. Not a wine, but a very strong dark beer with an intense, fruitlike malt and hop balance.

BELGIAN DUBBEL (DOUBLE). Rich and somewhat sweet, with a fruitlike aroma and very little bitterness.

BELGIAN STRONG DARK ALE. Not necessarily made in Belgium, this rich, often sweet, malty ale is high in alcohol. Hops are not dominant; instead, there's typically a spicy kick, a product of its distinct yeast.

BELGIAN STRONG PALE ALE. Complex and somewhat sweet, with an effervescent body.

BELGIAN WITBIER (WHITE BEER). A cloudy, easy-to-drink brew with a citrus aroma, a result of the yeast, which is typically unfiltered.

BROWN ALE. Roasty, nutty, and dark, with a light body.

DOUBLE IPA. Pumped-up India pale ale, with more malt, an extreme hop presence, and higher alcohol.

ENGLISH STRONG OR OLD ALE. Dark and somewhat malty, with a fruit character. Noticeable alcohol.

EXTRA SPECIAL BITTER (ESB). Medium hops bitterness, with a noticeable malt presence. Well balanced and very drinkable.

FRUIT BEER. Either an ale or a lager, typically sweetened with either fruit or fruit juice. Better versions tend to be tart, a result of fermentation with wild yeast.

IMPERIAL STOUT. Huge, powerfully malty body with a burnt, roasted flavor. High in alcohol, and ink-black in color.

INDIA PALE ALE (IPA). Pale golden in color, with an intense, herbal hop aroma and high bitterness.

PALE ALE. Pale in color and crisp tasting, often with grapefruitlike fruitiness. The Belgian version is less bitter.

PORTER. Dark, with a balanced bitterness. Frequently flavored with smoke or fruit.

SAISON OR BIÈRE DE GARDE. Golden- or orange-hued, with an intensely aromatic aroma and refreshing flavor. Bière de garde is stronger.

SCOTTISH ALE OR WEE HEAVY. Copper colored, sweet, and rich. with a full body, low hops, and some smokiness.

STOUT. Can be dry (Irish stout) or sweet (cream stout); American versions tend to be almost chocolatey. Oatmeal stout has a soft, smooth body.

WEIZENBOCK. A dark wheat beer with a spicy aroma and high alcohol.

WINTER WARMER. A moderately strong, dark ale with breadlike malt overtones. The spiced version is typically flavored with cinnamon, nutmeg, and cloves.

Lager

AMBER LAGER. Somewhat maltier than light lager, with little flavor of hops.

BOCK. A strong malt flavor with very light bitterness, somewhat warming. Dunkel bock is a dark bock.

DOPPELBOCK (DOUBLE BOCK). Typically darker than a bock, it's big, strong, and malty, with a roasted edge and high alcohol. A rare triple bock notches up both the malt and alcohol content.

HELLES. The German answer to Pilsner (it means "bright"), it's somewhat maltier, with lighter hops.

MARZEN. Copper-colored, full-bodied, and flavors of toast. A perfect accompaniment to many foods. Also known as Oktoberfest beer.

PILSNER. Bright, crisp, and clear, with a floral aroma and floral hops. Very refreshing.

VIENNA LAGER. A rich, toasted malt flavor, with light hops and light body.

❦ ACKNOWLEDGMENTS ❦

Lots of friends, colleagues, and beer folk got into the Christmas spirit and lent me a hand on this book.

Among the resources that provided important historical and technical help were BeerAdvocate.com, RateBeer.com, Nature.com, the Catholic Encyclopedia, The St. Nicholas Center, *All About Beer* magazine, the Newspaper Archives, the *New York Times*, the Brewers Association, and John Matthews's excellent book *The Winter Solstice: The Sacred Traditions of Christmas*.

Thanks also go to all the breweries that sent me samples of their beer—I drank every bit of it! Special thanks are due to Karl Stöhr from Schloss Eggenberg, who showed me everything I wanted to know about Samichlaus.

Fritz Maytag and Charles Finkel, two pioneers in America's craft beer movement, helped me greatly, as did Brian O'Reilly, Stephen Beaumont, Lucy Saunders, Jay Brooks, Knut Albert, Craig Hartinger, Daniel Shelton, Eduard Mollenkamp, Matthias Neidhart, Umit Ugur, Nima Hadain, Jeff Slick, Matt Guyer, Matt Capone, Horst Dornbusch, and Dale Van Wieren.

Clare Pelino and Jenny Hatton, my agents, held off my publisher while I tracked down all these great beers.

My brother, Bud Russell, a Baptist minister, often reminded me of everything I forgot from Sunday School. My longtime friend and colleague, Wayne Faircloth, photographed all the bottles—and didn't drink one! My wife, Theresa Conroy, trudged up and down Norway with me and encouraged me in every step of my work.

Finally, while I was writing this book, my friend, Beer Hunter Michael Jackson, passed away. I truly wanted him to read this because he provided more help and inspiration than I was ever able to thank him for.

INDEX

of Beers and Brewers

A

Aass Juleøl, 132
Abita Christmas Ale, 132
Achilles, 167
Achouffe, d', 156
Affligem Noël, 82
Ægir Julebrugg, 133
Alaskan Winter Ale, 118
Allagash Grand Cru, 133
Alpha Klaus, 88–89
Anchor, 25–27, 62–63
Anderson Valley, 68–69
Anheuser-Busch, 44–45, 155, 179
Anker, Het, 76
Appalachian, 144
Atwater Winter Bock, 134
Avec les Bons Voeux, 58–59
Avery, 70

B

Bad Elf, 45–46, 134
Bah Humbug, 135
Baladin Noël, 74–75
Baltimore-Washington, 161
Bavik, 112–13
Belgian Frostbite, 135
Bell's, 92–93
Bethlehem, 51–53, 162
Big Shot, 136
Binchoise Reserve Speciale, La, 77
Bink Winterkoninkske, 136
Blaugies, 152
Blue Point Winter Ale, 137
Boston, 117, 163, 164
Boulder, 156
Boulevard, 128–29
BridgePort, 96–97
Brooklyn Winter Ale, 137
Brown Shugga', 138

C

Celebration Ale, 64–65

Choulette de Noël, La, 98–99
Clay Pipe, 160
Clipper City, 109
Clootie Dumpling, 39
Coors, 178
Corsendonk Christmas Ale, 78–79
Criminally Bad Elf, 138
Cropton, 162
Cuvée Meilleurs Voeux, 139

D

Dahls Juleøl, 139
Delirium Noël, 72–73
Doggie Claws, 106–7
Dolle Brouwers, De, 61
Dominion Winter Brew, 140
Dragonne, La, 95
Dubuisson Frères, 91
Dupont, 58–59
Duyck, 103

E

Ebenezer Ale, 96–97
Eggenberg, 47–50, 60

F

Faust Winter Festbier, 141
Fish Tale WinterFish, 141
Flying Dog, 150
Flying Fish, 144
Föroya Bjór Jola Bryggj, 142
Fort Collins, 136
Franches-Montagnes, 95
Full Sail Wassail, 142
Fürst Carl Weihnachtsbock, 143
Fürstliches Brauhaus Ellingen, 143

G

Gale, George, 143
Geary's Winter Ale, 119
George Gale Christmas Ale, 143
Goose Island Christmas Ale, 110–11
Gouden Carolus Noël, 76

Grand Cru Winter Reserve, 144
Great Divide, 83
Great Lakes Christmas Ale, 145
Grinnin' Grizzly, 144

H
Haand, 157
Hacker-Pschorr Superior, 145
Hair of the Dog, 106–7
Hale's Ales Wee Heavy Winter Ale, 146
Harpoon Winter Warmer, 146
Harvey's Christmas Ale, 147
Heartland, 158
Heavy Seas Winter Storm, 109
He'brew Jewbelation, 41–42, 147
Herforder Weihnacht, 148
Hibernation Ale, 83
High Falls, 140
High Point, 160
Hitachino Nest Commemorative Ale, 104–5
Hofbräu Festbier, 148
Hook Norton, 173
Hoppy Holidaze Flavored Ale, 149
Huyghe, 72–73

I
Isolation Ale, 149

J
Jenlain Noël, 103
Jolly Pumpkin Artisan Ales, 157
JW Dundee's Special Edition Festival Ale, 140

K
Kaltenberg, 152
Kerkom, 136
Kerstmutske Christmas Nightcap, 150
Kerst Pater, 116
Kiuchi, 104–5
Klaster Winter Lager, 151
Klein Duimpje Kerstbier, 151
K-9 Cruiser, 150
Koch's Holiday Beer, 27–28
König Ludwig Festtags-Bier, 152
Koninck, De, 177
Kulmbacher, 130

L
Lagunitas, 138
Lakefront Holiday Spice, 153

Lancaster Winter Warmer, 153
Left Hand, 168
Lion, The, 170
Longfellow Winter Ale, 114–15
Lump of Coal, 154

M
Mack Juleøl, 154
Mad Elf, 56–57
Magic Hat, 161
Mahr's Christmas Bock, 80–81
Marin, 149
Matt, 166, 167
Meckatzer Fest-Märzen, 155
Michelob Celebrate, 155
Middle Ages, 180
Mikkeller, 165
Miller Special Christmas Beer, 27
Mönchshof Weihnachtsbier, 130
Moneuse Special Winter Ale, La, 152
Moylan's, 176

N
Never Summer Ale, 156
New Belgium, 94
N'ice Chouffe, 156
Nissemor, 157
Noel de Calabaza, 157
Nøgne Ø Winter Ale (God Jul), 158
Nutcracker Ale, 128–29

O
Odell, 149
Old Dominion, 140
Old Jubilation, 70
Old Man Winter Ale, 124
Old Red Nose, 158
Otter Creek Winter Ale, 159
Our Special Ale, 26–27, 62–63

P
Paper City, 178
Pennsylvania, 100–101
Père Noël, 122–23
Petrus Winterbeer, 112–13
Port, 165
Prelude Special Ale, 159
Proef, De, 150
Pursuit of Happiness, 160
Pyramid, 127

R

Ramstein Winter Wheat, 160
Ranke, De, 122–23
Raven Christmas Lager, The, 161
Red Hook, 179
Regenboog, De, 125
Ridgeway, 45–46, 134, 138, 154, 164, 173, 175
Ringnes Julebokk, 71
River Horse, 135
Rogue Ales, 84–85
Roxy Rolles, 161
Rude Elf's Reserve, 51–53, 162
Rudolph's Revenge, 162
Rulles, La, 139

S

Saint Arnold Christmas Ale, 163
St. Bernardus Christmas Ale, 108
St. Feuillien Cuvée de Noël, 102
St. Nikolaus Bock Bier, 100–101
Samichlaus Bier, 47–50, 60
Samuel Adams Holiday Porter, 163
Samuel Adams Old Fezziwig, 117
Samuel Adams Winter Lager, 164
Samuel Smith's Winter Welcome Ale, 66–67
Santa's Butt, 45–46, 164
Santa's Little Helper (Mikkeller), 165
Santa's Little Helper (Port), 165
Santa's Private Reserve Ale, 84–85
Saranac Chocolate Amber, 166
Saranac Season's Best, 166
Saranac Winter Wassail, 167
Scaldis Noël, 91
Schell, August, 169
Schmaltz, 41–42, 147
Senne, De La, 180
Serafijn Christmas Angel, 167
Shipyard, 114–15, 159
Sierra Nevada, 64–65
Slaapmutske, 150
Sly Fox Christmas Ale, 168
Smisje Kerst, 't, 125
Smith, Samuel, 66
Smuttynose Winter Ale, 86–87
SnowBound Winter Ale, 168
Snow Cap, 127
Snow Goose Winter Ale, 120–21
SnowStorm, 169
Southern Tier, 124
Spanish Peaks, 177

Sprecher Winter Brew, 169
Stegmaier Holiday Warmer, 170
Stille Nacht, 61
Stoudt's Winter Ale, 170
Summit Winter Ale, 171

T

Three Floyds, 88–89
Thurn and Taxis Winter Festbier, 171
Tommyknocker Cocoa Porter, 172
Tröegs, 56–57
Tuborg Weihnachts Pilsener, 172
Twelve Days, 173
2° Below Ale, 94

V

Van den Bossche, 116
Very Bad Elf, 45, 173
Vestfyen Julebrugg, 174
Vifilfell, 174
Viking Jólabjór, 174

W

Walter's Holiday Beer, 28
Warm Welcome, 175
Weeping Radish Christmas Beer, 175
Well's & Young's, 126
Weltenberger Kloster, 90
Weyerbacher Winter Ale, 176
White Christmas, 176
Wild Goose, 120–21
Winter Cheer, 177
Winterfest, 178
Winter Hook, 179
Winter Koninck, 177
Winter Palace Wee Heavy, 178
Winter's Bourbon Cask Ale, 179
Winter Solstice, 68–69
Winter-Traum, 90
Winter White Ale, 92–93
Wizard's Winter Ale, 180
Wychwood, 135

Y

Young's Winter Warmer, 126

Z

Zinnebir X-Mas, 180